LOYALIST LISTS

*Over 2000 Loyalist Names and Families
from the Haldimand Papers*

E. Keith Fitzgerald

This publication was financially assisted in part by a Wintario Program Grant from the Ontario Ministry of Citizenship and Culture.

Cover art by Barbara Podor.

Back cover: The coming of the Loyalists, 1783. By Henry Sandham.
(PAC, Negative C-168)

I.S.B.N. 0-920036-03-1

CONTENTS

Transcribed by
E. Keith Fitzgerald, M.D.
December 1983.

---

* In 1784, the Province of Quebec included present day Ontario.

** "Upper Posts" likely referred to military posts up-stream from Montreal, i.e., in present day Ontario.

*** The brevity of 1KRRNY Roll could be as a result of some Companies being posted at the "Upper Posts", i.e., outside Montreal area.

PREFACE

It is an axiom of genealogical research that the best record for the researcher to use is the record of the event, created at the time it occurred. These transcripts fit that description perfectly:

a. "General Return of Refugee Loyalists in the Province of Quebec";

b. "Roll of King's Rangers";

c. "Return of the 1st Battalion of the King's Royal Regiment of New York (1KRRNY)"; and

d. "Return of Loyal Rangers – Company of Pensioners (Jessup's)".

Another axiom of genealogical research is that an official record is preferable to private or other less official records. The reasoning is that officialdom has no bias one way or the other. Of course, that is not always true, and the official, being "disinterested", is more prone to mistakes of spelling and other detail. These returns and roll are no exception.

In the case of the Haldimand Papers, it must be remembered that Sir Frederick Haldimand was the governor of the Province of Quebec during almost the whole period of the Revolutionary War, seven and a half years from the spring of 1777, when Carleton resigned the governorship, until November 1784, when Haldimand sailed for London on a leave of absence. The government of that time was centred entirely on Haldimand and his immediate entourage. There was no Legislative Assembly, as such, nor any substantial bureaucracy, so that all correspondence was directed to and from the governor/commander-in-chief and his personal aides; and private citizens could and did address themselves directly to government, through him and his staff. In addition, the infrastructure of the Province was extremely rudimentary, so that all the provisioning required to prosecute a war and resettle a displaced people came directly under Haldimand's supervision; hence the origin of the returns and roll transcribed and indexed here.

It has been suggested that the interested researcher can read these returns and roll directly from the microfilms at the Public Archives of Canada (PAC) or from microfilms on interlibrary loan from the PAC. In his introduction, Dr. Fitzgerald states that "The (PAC) copy provided for transcription is well written and quite easy to read...." That may be true for the PAC copy; however, the World Microfilms Publications, 62 Queen's Grove, London NW8 6ER England has the commercial rights to reproduction of the Haldimand Collection, and its version of this portion of the film is very faint and difficult to read. In addition, the interlibrary system, so dear to the genealogist's heart, is not notably quick, and the researcher has only a limited amount of time to use the loaned microfilm. Copies of PAC microfilms can be purchased, but if the research involves several films, that route can become rather expensive.

Also, in his introduction, Dr. Fitzgerald points out the problem of accessing the appropriate record, due to confusion over the way the Collection has been catalogued. Even using the guide to the 115-reel World Microfilm edition as well as the PAC reports more detailed cataloguing of the Collection accessing the appropriate return of roll is more serendipitous than systematic.

In conclusion then, this "personal memorial project of the 200th Anniversary of the arrival of the Loyalists in Ontario, c1784", by Dr. E. Keith Fitzgerald, is a valuable addition to the ever-growing store of "official records" of Quebec's or Canada's first years as a separate province, severed from the lost British Empire to the South, particularly because of its time-saving index. Dr. Fitzgerald is to be commended for his effort in this trailblazing project to make information from the Haldimand Papers more available to researchers.

James Zavits

LOYALIST LISTS:
OVER 2000 LOYALIST NAMES AND FAMILIES
FROM THE HALDIMAND[1] PAPERS

INTRODUCTION
As a personal project to commemorate the year 1984 — the 200th Anniversary of the coming of the Loyalists to what became the Province of Ontario — an amateur genealogist presents his transcription of some of the Loyalist Lists found in the Haldimand Papers. The assistance of the Public Archives of Canada (PAC) is gratefully acknowledged; in particular, the help of Brian Driscoll of the British Archives, Manuscript Division, Archives Branch of PAC is mentioned. Copyright release from The British Library was received under their letter RAHS/DAW of 16 September, 1983.

REFERENCE
The Canadian holdings at PAC are under Call Number — Great Britain, Add. Mss. 21826. This same Call Number would be used if one wished to check the originals in the British Library. Microfilm copies are available on interlibrary loan.

TRANSCRIBER'S NOTES TO AID IN UTILIZATION
1. The four parts are undated. One might speculate as to the likely dates of the various parts to make them more useful, but that is subject to inherent inaccuracies. It is sufficient to date them as likely sometime in 1784 as the Nominal Roll of 1KRRNY is considerably shorter than the one of their disbandment on 24 December, 1783 at Lachine, Quebec. Indeed, it is shorter than that of JESSUP'S RANGERS — a much smaller unit of the Provincials. Additionally, Haldimand left Canada in 1784; consequently, these lists could not be any later than that year.

2. The copy provided for transcription is well written and quite easy to read. Less than 3% of the original letters are subject to more than one interpreta-

---

[1] Sir Frederick Haldimand (1718-1791), a Swiss mercenary and close friend of Henry Bouquet (see Add. Mss. 21631-21660), entered the British Army in 1756 and served with considerable distinction through the period of upheaval in North America which included the Seven Years' War and the American Revolution. Haldimand arrived at New York in June 1756 with a lieutenant-colonel's commission in the Royal American Regiment. In 1758, he joined Major-General James Abercromby's expedition against Canada, which failed at the cost of great bloodshed at Ticonderoga. In the following year, Haldimand conducted a distinguished defence of Oswego, and joined Major-General Jeffrey Amherst's expedition against Montreal in 1760. After serving at Trois-Rivières as commander, and as acting governor, he was transferred to Florida. Recalled to England in 1775, he returned to Canada in 1778 and succeeded Sir Guy Carleton as governor and commander-in-chief. In 1784, he left for England on leave of absence, but never returned to his post, and retired in 1786. The Haldimand Papers, which include official correspondence and records of his various commands at Trois-Rivières, Florida, New York and Quebec, were presented to the British Museum in 1857 by philanthropist William Haldimand (1784-1862), nephew and heir of Sir Frederick. The first Dominion (of Canada) Archivist, Douglas Brymner, initiated in 1879 a transcription programme, which was completed by 1888. In addition, the originals were microfilmed between 1966 and 1969.

tion, e.g., "N", "U", "i" and "e". Spelling errors abound — but are faithfully reproduced. One suspects that the lists were written by a variety of clerks at various locations — then consolidated into the journal by one scribe. There is ample evidence of the use of phonetic spellings of some of the names by the clerks. As a result, users are urged to consider as wide a range of spellings of the names of their interest as possible. If the writer were to interpret and correct the spelling errors, he would be forcing his interpretation of what he thinks the clerk meant to write onto the reader, e.g., "McENTIRE" is copied but obviously it could be spelled "McINTYRE". And this is by English clerks of Anglo-Saxon names. Consider the reverse aspect. In the NYG&B RECORD 114:63 (1983) is a baptismal list of a Lutheran Church where the Pastor wrote in German:

"1764 – 16ten Mertz JOHN MECKENTHEYER und seine frau CATHERINA, MARIA (their daughter with sponsors) MERPHI MECKENTHEYER und seine frau ELISABETH".

One can easily interpret this as another spelling of "McINTYRE". (Note the German spelling of ELIZABETH).

3. Alphabetization is difficult and every effort is made to give as many possible spellings in the index. In cases such as "THOMAS ANDREW" both names are indexed as surnames.

4. Not reproduced are the florid initials, "LSD", that appear on each page at the top right beside the word "Remarks". Other differences from the original are:

   a. The left-hand column, "NUMBER", has been added for indexing purposes.

   b. Some pages had columns entitled "UNINCORPORATED MEN" and "INCORPORATED MEN" and others did not; these columns appear consistently throughout the transcription so as not to confuse the reader. Notes have been used to explain if these columns exist or not on a particular page. PART IV is in a different format from the other PARTS.

   c. The writing in the column "From What Province or Country" was vertical in the original; it has been placed horizontally to ease reading. On some pages the word "Country" is written "County".

   d. The words "End fo. --- (p. ---)" do not appear in the original but have been added to assist the reader.

5. Liberal use has been made of footnotes to assist the reader and to supply supplemental information.

6. Abbreviations of titles and names are as in the original. "Mrs" is as used for Mrs.; military rank titles are varied. An interesting abbreviation variation is found for what is likely "JOHN" or "JOHANNES". The writer had pre-

viously learned that JOHN was abbreviated "J^{no}" — but mostly this abbreviation is clearly written "J^{ns}", even when also clearly preceded by "J^{no}" at the bottom of the preceding page. What is not understandable is why the abbreviation was used at all when there was ample space to write "JOHN" as happened on many occasions and the space was so used. The transcriber speculates that "J^{no}" was JOHN; and that "J^{ns}" was meant for JOHANNES. Then there are the whims of the clerks.

7. The individual pages have been given numbers using a rubber stamp — likely by the Archivists. The numbers used are 197 to 251. The original clerks used the term "fo." for Folios as these were in a bound journal. Each sheet of paper had a folio number, e.g., "fo. 143"; when the sheet was on the right-hand side of the journal it was labelled "fo. 143" and when the sheet was turned over, and was now on the left-hand side of the journal, it was labelled "143^v" — the "v" standing for "verso" or reverse or left-hand.

8. Note that the arithmetic and additions of the clerks has not been checked except in a few obvious cases; there are some errors.

9. There is no obvious explanation for some families drawing rations and others not. The ration allowance would appear to be one per adult man or male over 12; a half ration for a woman and some of the older children with a quarter ration for younger children. There were some variations on this, however, as some women are noted to get a full ration, specially if unaccompanied — pregnancy?

10. There are approximately two typewritten pages to each original handwritten page — if the original was full.

11. The transcriber's family of prime interest is the EMPEYs. From known information about that family some extrapolations can be made that may help or confuse the reader. That all possible names are not included is deduced from the fact that Sgt. ADAM P. EMPEY'S name is missing. He was b. 16 Apr 1755 per Stone Arabia Trinity Lutheran Church in Palatine (SATL); he m. ALLADA (OLIVE) HARE, wid/o Lt. HENRY HARE, and served in 1KRRNY from 15 Aug 1777. Also missing is his brother, Private JACOBUS EMPEY, b. 7 Apr 1763 (SATL) — both sons of PHILIP Snr. Thus, the reader should not put too much credence in the lack of some names from these lists.

12. Some of the Part I names suggest these men were serving at one time in the Provincial Forces — though the writer is not as familiar with these names as those of 1KRRNY. However, the writer believes many of these names were to be found in later years around Brockville, Ontario and Prince Edward County (west of Kingston in the area of Belleville). Some are names of Loyalists found in the Maritimes. BUELL is a Brockville name; JOHN FITZGERALD is a name found to have settled north of Brockville. The name BRISBIN is to be found to-day in Kingston and this was the name of

an Army house occupied by the writer in the late 1960s — just east of Vimy Barracks on Highway No. 2. A descendant of one of the BRISBINs on these lists likely named that house.

13. The reader will note the clerk's habit of recording the first name/word on the following folio at the bottom right hand corner of the preceding page.

14. The expression in the Remarks Column "Gone to the Colonies" could be interpreted as the Maritimes, the West Indies or return to the States; whichever it means is unknown. Some are known to have gone on their lands in Ontario.

15. There are many more lists waiting to be copied at the PAC Haldimand Papers.

The following is an extract from a letter by John E. Ruch dated 9 August 1984 to Dr. E. Keith Fitzgerald regarding this manuscript, and in particular, concerning entries No. 114 and 115.

"... The dating of the Refugee List, Hald. Pprs. 21,826 ff. 143-170, or at least a good part of it can be seen to be shortly after the first week in Sept. 1783. The clue is on f.144ᵛ. ELIAS SMITH (No. 114) and MOSES SHERWOOD (No. 115) "lately from New York". The remark to me means that they had only just recently come in. Their ship, "Industry", made port at Quebec City early in Sept. It should be possible to date that, and their departure for upstream quarters. CUYLER and DeCOIGNE were compiling returns at the camps during Sept. Larry Turner does not deal with this particular shipload, but concentrates on the groups with P. VAN ALSTINE and M. GRASS in his book *Voyage of a Different Kind* (Mika Publishing Co., Belleville, Ont.) and gives rolls for them".

COMMENT
This is of course pure speculation in an attempt to date these lists. John Ruch is undoubtedly correct in the arrival of the "Industry" at Quebec City — but how long did these two men dally at Quebec before leaving for Montreal? All this does is confirm that the lists are dated *after* September 1783 and before May/June 1784.

JOHN E. RUCH is an author of authoritative Loyalist articles (see *Canadian Genealogist* 5:30, March 1983) and President of a UEL Association Branch. In another letter dated 7 Feb 1984, he comments that ELIAS SMITH "embarked at NYC on 25 Aug 1783".

EKF Aug 1984

PART I

General Return of Refugee Loyalists in the Province of Quebec,
exclusive of those Quartered, and residing at the Upper Posts

Folios 143 to 153^V; names No. 1 to 787

1

General Return of Refugee Loyalists in the Province of Quebec, Exclusive of those Quartered, and residing at the Upper Posts

NUMBER	NAMES	UNINCORPORATED MEN	INCORPORATED MEN	WOMEN	CHILDREN MALE ABOVE 12 YEARS	CHILDREN MALE BETWEEN 12 & 6 YEARS	CHILDREN MALE UNDER 6 YEARS	CHILDREN FEMALE ABOVE 12 YEARS	CHILDREN FEMALE BETWEEN 12 & 6 YEARS	CHILDREN FEMALE UNDER 6 YEARS	TOTAL	Nº RATIONS PR DAY	FROM WHAT PROVINCE OR COUNTRY	REMARKS
1	Barnet Mrs			1	1	1			1		4	1 3/4	New York	
2	Bastedo Jacob		**	1	2	1	3				8	1		
3	Blunt Margt			1							1	1		
4	Crookshanks Wm.	1		1		1			1	2	6	3	New York	Merchant
5	Cruthers Mrs			2		1			2		5	2 1/2	Do	a widow pensioned
6	Carr Mrs			1		1					2	1 1/2		
7	Campbell Mrs			1	1	3		1	2		8	3	New York	a widow
8	Cromp Thomas	1									1	1		
9	Cartwright Mrs			1			1		1		3	1 1/2	Do	
10	Carson Thomas	1		1		1					3	1 1/2		
11	Cameron John	1		1							2	1 1/2		
12	Carman Micheal*	1		1							2	1 1/2		
13	Cough John	1		1	2	2					6	1 1/2		
14	Campbell Alexr	1		1	2	2	3		1		9	4	New York	formerly a Justice of Peace now Innholder at Montreal
15	Costello Cathr			1	1		1	1			4	3/4		
16	Deforest Mrs			1	1		1	2	2	1	6	2 1/2	New York	a widow
17	Falkner Ralph	1		2	1	1		1	1		5	2 3/4	Do	Farmer & wheelwright
18	Fisher John	1		1	4			1			7	1 1/2	Do	
19	Grant Robert	1		1	2	1		1	1		7	2 1/2	Do	Baker
20	Gibbins Mary			1			1	1			3	1 1/2	Do	
21	Hiks Paul	1		1	2	1		2			6	2	Do	Farmer
22	Hogle Frances			1	2	2	1	1	2		8	1 3/4		
23	Hair Margerit			(a)	1		1		3		4	2	New York	a Widow Pensioned

NOTES: * = sic = as written
             ** = This column does not appear in the original.
             (a) = No woman shown

fo. 143

NUMBER	NAMES	UNINCORPORATED MEN	INCORPORATED MEN	WOMEN	Male Above 12	Male Between 12 & 6	Male Under 6	Female Above 12	Female Between 12 & 6	Female Under 6	TOTAL	N° RATIONS PR DAY	FROM WHAT PROVINCE OR COUNTRY	REMARKS
							CHILDREN							
24	Hicks Mrs			1	2	2	1	1	1		8	1 3/4		
25	Hendrick Elizabeth			1							1	1/2		
26	Kenedy William*	1		1		2	2		2		8	4		
27	Kemble Barbara			1				1	1		3	1		
28	Logan James	1									1	1	New York	Baker
29	McDonel* Angus				1			1	1		2	1/2		
30	Miller Thomas	1		1	4			1	1		8	2	New York	Farmer
31	McCoristine Terence	1		1		1		1	1		4	2 1/4	New York	Do
32	Miller Peter	1		1		2		2	1		5	1 1/2	Do	
33	McIntosh Donald	1		1		1		1	1	1	7	3	Do	
34	Morden Lorina			1			1	1			3	1/2	Do	
35	Munro Nancy			1							1	1/2		
36	McDonel* Ketty Junr*			1				1	1		3	3/4		
37	McDonel* Ketty Junr*			1							2	1		
	End fo. 143 (p. 197)													
	Carried Over	20		36	26	22	14	20	23	5	166	62 1/4		McDonel

NOTES: Nos. 36 & 37 are identical in the "NAMES" column.

3

NUMBER	NAMES	UNINCORPORATED MEN	INCORPORATED MEN	WOMEN	CHILDREN MALE ABOVE 12 YEARS	MALE BETWEEN 12 & 6 YEARS	MALE UNDER 6 YEARS	FEMALE ABOVE 12 YEARS	FEMALE BETWEEN 12 & 6 YEARS	FEMALE UNDER 6 YEARS	TOTAL	Nº RATIONS PR DAY	FROM WHAT PROVINCE OR COUNTRY	REMARKS
	Brought Forward	20	**	36	26	22	14	20	23	5	166	62 1/4		
38	McDonel Nelly			1						1	2	1		
39	Man John	1		1						1	3	1		
40	Man Isaac	1									1			
41	Parker William			1	2	3	1	1		1	9	3 1/4	New York	Cordwainer
42	Pruiner Peter	1		1	1		1	3			7	1 3/4	Do	Farmer
43	Pickin Mrs			1	1	2		1			5	1	Do	a widow
44	Robertson Thoms	1		1	2	1		1	1		7	2		
45	Rose Elizabeth			1					2		3	1 1/4		
46	Robeson Susana			(a)		1					2	1/2		
47	Skimming Mary			1	2					2	5	2 1/2		
48	Scott Walter	1		1	1	1	1	3			8	3	New York	Farmer
49	Schilling John	1		1		1		1			4	1 1/2	New York	
50	Singer John	1									1	1		
51	Semour Sarah			1		1	1				3	1		
52	Tibere Joseph	1		1			2		1		5	1 1/2	New York	Farmer
53	Mary Donally			1							1			
54	Van Vorst Jns	1									1	(b)		
55	Vandeker Rudoff	1		1	1	1			1	1	6	1	New York	gone to the Colonies
56	Waldroff Margt			1				2	1		4	2 1/4	Do	Farmer
57	Wait John	1									1	1 1/2	Do	
58	Sophy Matyce			1							1	1/2	Do	
59	Robert Petyerew	1										1		
60	Thomas Andrews	1		1	1	1	1	2	2	1	10	2 1/2	New York	Farmer

NOTES: (b) = no rations shown
No. 42 Peter PRUNER ? A PETER PRUNER allotted Lot 15w Concession II, 3rd (Osnabruck) Twsp.
No. 59 PETTIGREW ?

4

NUMBER	NAMES	UNINCORPORATED MEN	INCORPORATED MEN	WOMEN	CHILDREN MALE ABOVE 12 YEARS	CHILDREN MALE BETWEEN 12 & 6 YEARS	CHILDREN MALE UNDER 6 YEARS	CHILDREN FEMALE ABOVE 12 YEARS	CHILDREN FEMALE BETWEEN 12 & 6 YEARS	CHILDREN FEMALE UNDER 6 YEARS	TOTAL	Nº RATIONS PR DAY	FROM WHAT PROVINCE OR COUNTRY	REMARKS
61	Fredrick Hass	1									1	1		
62	Michael Gates	1		1			1		3		6	3 1/4		
63	Mrs Sutherland			1					1		2	1		
64	Matty Stanly	1		1		1	1			1	5	1 1/2	Vermount*	
65	Mrs Wolent			1							1	1 1/2	New York	Farmer
66	Joseph Couckhill	1					2	2			5	1	Do	Carpenter
67	Mrs Embury			1			1		1		3	1	Do	Farmer
68	Peter Van Camp	1				1				1	2	1/2	Do	
69	Jenny McWilliams			1					1		2	1/2		
70	Simon Van Camp	1				1			1	1	2	3/4		
71	Peter Garlock	1									1	1/2		
72	Mrs Vanalstine			1		2				1	6	2		Mary
	End fo. 143ᵛ (p. 198)													
	Carried Over	38		60	39	40	25	37	38	14	291	109 3/4		

NOTES: No. 72 – see Nos. 164, 676, 1144 & 1224. In a British Military map drawn during the French and Indian War and dated 1757 the house of "Van Alstyn" is clearly shown on the south bank of the Mohawk River just east of Canajoharie Creek (35 miles west of Schenectady).

NUMBER	NAMES	MEN UNINCORPORATED	INCORPORATED MEN	WOMEN	CHILDREN MALE ABOVE 12 YEARS	CHILDREN MALE BETWEEN 12 & 6 YEARS	CHILDREN MALE UNDER 6 YEARS	CHILDREN FEMALE ABOVE 12 YEARS	CHILDREN FEMALE BETWEEN 12 & 6 YEARS	CHILDREN FEMALE UNDER 6 YEARS	TOTAL	No RATIONS PR DAY	FROM WHAT PROVINCE OR COUNTRY	REMARKS
	Brought Forward	38	(c)	60	39	40	25	37	38	14	291	109 3/4		
73	Mary Campbell			1					1		4	1/2		
74	Elizabeth Bowman			1		1			2	1	3	1 3/4		
75	Mrs McDonel widow			1		2		2	1		6	1/2		
76	John Wood	1			1						7	2 3/4	New York	Farmer
77	Mary Philips	1		1			1			3	1	2 1/4	Do	Mill Wright
78	Nicholas Simons	1									2	1	Do	Farmer
79	Renold McDonel	1			1						2	1/2		
80	Mrs Platt			1							4	1 1/2	New York	a Widow Pensioned
81	Mrs McLarin	1		1			1			2	2	1/2		
82	Mrs Murkeson	1		1		1					3	2	New York	Baker
83	Jaspar Honer	1				1					6	1		
84	Joseph Hanes & Fambly	1		1	1			3			5	1		
85	Amy Terry	1		1			1			2	2	1/2	New York	
86	Henry Winter	1									5	1 1/2		
87	Mrs Granes widow & children			2			2				(d)	1 1/2	New York	
88	Thomas Cavan	1		1		2	1				5			
89	Robert Garrit	1		1	1	1			1	1	6	(b)	New York	Farmer
90	Duncan Reed	1		1					1		2	(b)	Do	Do
91	Alexr Fisher	1		1							3	(b)	Do	
92	Thomas Partridge	1		1							2	(b)	Do	Farmer
93	Duncan Fisher	1		1							2	(b)	New York	Farmer
94	Alexr McCan	1									1	(b)	New York	Farmer

NOTES: (c) = This column appears on this page and is not used. The empty column is immediately next to the names column in the original.
(d) = No entry

NUMBER	NAMES	UNINCORPORATED MEN	INCORPORATED MEN	WOMEN	MALE ABOVE 12 YEARS	MALE BETWEEN 12 & 6 YEARS	MALE UNDER 6 YEARS	FEMALE ABOVE 12 YEARS	FEMALE BETWEEN 12 & 6 YEARS	FEMALE UNDER 6 YEARS	TOTAL	N° RATIONS PR DAY	FROM WHAT PROVINCE OR COUNTRY	REMARKS
95	John Anna	1		1						1	3	(b)	Do	Farmer
96	Nathaniel Starns	1		1	2	2					6	(b)	Do	
97	John Orr	1									1	(b)		
98	James Campbell	1									1	(b)		
99	James Hall	1			1						1	(b)		
100	Harmanns Flock	1		1	1	1					4	(b)	New York	
101	Rosana Short	1					2	2			5	(b)	New York	Farmer
102	Conrad Sales	1									1	(b)	Do	Do
103	Isreal* Osburn	1									1	(b)	Do	Do
104	Alexr. Osburn	1		1							2	(b)	Do	Do
105	Bt. Dyer	1				2					3	1 1/2		
106	Dedrick Friday	1							1		1	(b)	New York	
107	Rachael Knight	1							1		1	(b)	Do	
108	Stephen Brown	1					1				2	(b)	Do	
109	David Wiles	1									1	(b)		
110	William Timmer	1									1	1		gone to the Colonies
111	Jns Coughnot ***	1									1	1		
112	Mary Grant	1		1							2	(b)		Donald
	End fo. 144 (p. 199)													
	Carried Over	67		87	47	54	34	44	46	24	403	134		

NOTES: *** A famous Loyalist surname, usually written Van Koughnet. Believed to have settled in Prince Edward County and ancestor of a current Member of Parliament.

NUMBER	NAMES	UNINCORPORATED MEN	INCORPORATED MEN	WOMEN	CHILDREN MALE Above 12 Years	Male Between 12 & 6 Years	Male Under 6 Years	FEMALE Above 12 Years	Female Between 12 & 6 Years	Female Under 6 Years	TOTAL	No RATIONS PR DAY	FROM WHAT PROVINCE OR COUNTRY	REMARKS
	Brought forward	67	(c)	87	47	54	34	44	46	24	403	134		
113	Donald Fisher	1		1	2						4	(b)	New York	lately from New York
114	Elias Smith	1		1	2	2		3		2	11	3		Ditto
115	Moses Sherwood	1		1			2	1	1	3	9	2 3/4		Lately from N. York & vessel
116	Joseph Bragley	1		1		1		3			6	2		Master of a vessel
117	Andrew Abrahams	1		1	1						3	1 1/2	New York	Do
118	Cornelius Ryan	1		1	1						3	1 1/2	Do	
119	Adam Stocks	1									1	1 3/4	Do	
120	Jacob Bears	1									1	1	Do	
121	George Fellers	1		1							2	1	Do	
122	Laurence Emery	1		1			1			2	5	(b)	Do	Cordwainer
123	Isaac Montross	1		1							2	(b)	Do	
124	Lewis Nedo	1		1			1				3	(b)	Do	Baker
125	Duncan McGregor	1		1							2	(b)	Do	
126	James Rough	1									1	(b)		
127	William Smith	1									1	(b)		
128	Thomas Munro	1									1	(b)		
129	Finley Ross	1									1	(b)		
130	Elizabeth Munro			1							1	(b)		
131	James Young	1									1	(b)	New York	
132	Mary McIntosh			1							1	(b)		
133	Solomon Beacher	1									1	(b)	New York	
134	Nicholas Stoneman	1		1							2	(b)		Carpenter

NOTES:

8

NUMBER	NAMES	UNINCORPORATED MEN	INCORPORATED MEN	WOMEN	CHILDREN MALE ABOVE 12 YEARS	MALE BETWEEN 12 & 6 YEARS	MALE UNDER 6 YEARS	FEMALE ABOVE 12 YEARS	FEMALE BETWEEN 12 & 6 YEARS	FEMALE UNDER 6 YEARS	TOTAL	N° RATTIONS PR DAY	FROM WHAT PROVINCE OR COUNTRY	REMARKS
136	William McCough	1		1					1		3	(b)	Connecticutt*	Farmer
137	Ephriem Airs	1									1	(b)		
138	Jⁿˢ Campbell	1									1	(b)		
139	Peter Milhanch	1									1	(b)		
140	William Stuard *	1									1	(b)		
141	Daniel Robinson	1									1	(b)		
142	George Wait	1									1	(b)		
143	Major Watson (s?)	1		1							2	(b)		
144	Susan McInly			1							1	(b)		
145	Jⁿˢ Roach	1									1	(b)		
146	Jⁿˢ Gooniff 1	1			1						1	(b)		
147	William England	1		1	1						3	(b)		
148	Amos Ansley	1									2	(b)		Carpenter
149	Jⁿˢ Stuard *	1			1						1	(b)		
150	Susan Dunbar	1		1							3	(b)	New York	
151	Mⁿ Adams	1		1							2	(b)	Do	Farmer & Innkeeper
152	Joseph Higgins	1		1							1	(b)	Do	
153	Mealin Knight	1									1	(b)		Archibald
	End fo. 144ᵛ (p. 200)													
	Carried Over	103		107	54	57	38	53	49	32	493	148 1/2		

NOTES: 1. 2nd choice Goonoff.

9

NUMBER	NAMES	UNINCORPORATED MEN	INCORPORATED MEN	WOMEN	CHILDREN MALE ABOVE 12 YEARS	MALE BETWEEN 12 & 6 YEARS	MALE UNDER 6 YEARS	FEMALE ABOVE 12 YEARS	FEMALE BETWEEN 12 & 6 YEARS	FEMALE UNDER 6 YEARS	TOTAL	No RATIONS PR DAY	FROM WHAT PROVINCE OR COUNTRY	REMARKS
	Brought Forward	103	(c)	107	54	57	38	53	49	32	493	148 1/2	New York	
154	Archibald Hall	1		1							2	(b)	Do	
155	William Creighton	1		1							2	(b)	Do	
156	George Crawford	1		1							2	(b)	Do	
157	David Foster	1									1	(b)	Do	
158	Ralph Criste *	1									1	(b)	Do	
159	John Gibson	1		1							2	(b)	Do	Taylor
160	Robert McDonel	1									1	(b)	Do	
161	Elizabeth Winter			1							1	(b)		
162	John Deatlor	1			2						3	(b)	New York	Farmer
163	Frances Waggoner	1		1		2	1	1	2	1	8	(b)	Do	Painter
164	Margt Vanalstine			1							1	(b)		
165	Donald Wilkison 2	1				1			1		1	(b)	New York	Farmer
166	Aron Bratt	1				3			2		2	(b)	Do	Do
167	Hugh Cameron	1				1					5	(b)	Do	
168	Malcolm McMartin	1		1		1	2	1		1	6	(b)		
169	Mrs. Herkiman			1	2		1				5	3	New York	Cooper
170	Thimoty * Buell	1		1		1					4	(b)		
171	Mrs Culbert			1		1					4	1 1/2		
172	James Forsythe			1		1					2	1 1/2		
173	Mrs Wartman			1		2					6	1		
174	Mr Simmons			1				3			4	1 1/2		
175	Mr McNairne			1			1		1	1	2	1 1/2		
176	Hargo Johnston			1							2	3/4		

NOTES: 2. 2nd choice Wilkinson.

No. 164 - see Nos 72, 676, 1144, & 1224.

No. 170 - a famous Brockville, Ont. surname.

No. 169 - Wife of General HERCHHEIMER the American hero of the Battle of Oriskany 6 August, 1777 ? She left him and located in Kingston, Ontario with their children where she spelled her name HERCHMER. Gen. NICOLAUS HERCHHEIMER's family changed the spelling to HERKIMER, as the County, named for him, is spelled.

NUMBER	NAMES	UNINCORPORATED MEN	INCORPORATED MEN	WOMEN	CHILDREN MALE ABOVE 12 YEARS	MALE BETWEEN 12 & 6 YEARS	MALE UNDER 6 YEARS	FEMALE ABOVE 12 YEARS	FEMALE BETWEEN 12 & 6 YEARS	FEMALE UNDER 6 YEARS	TOTAL	No RATIONS PR DAY	FROM WHAT PROVINCE OR COUNTRY	REMARKS
177	Ralph Falkner	1		1			1			1	1	1	New York	Farmer
178	Cloe Frost			1						1	2	(b)	Vermont*	
179	Mary Muchmore			1			1				2	(b)		
180	Anderson James	1		1			1				3	1/2		
181	Brown Jesse Junr			1		1					1	1		
182	Buck Widow			1					1		1	1/2		
183	Babeety Mrs			1							4	2		
184	Bremer George Senr	1		1		3	1				8	2 1/2	New York	Farmer
185	Brisbin William	1		1	2		1				2	3 3/4	Do	
186	Batise Widow			1							1	1/2		
187	Bennit Ephraim			1							1	1/2		
189	Burrons Thomas			1	1	2					4	1 1/2		
190	Loveless Mrs			1										
	End fo. 145 (p. 201)													
	Inserted as an omission													
188	Patrick Smith Esq. (proper placement is between No. 710 & 711)	1			1						2	(b)		formerly Justice of the Peace
	Carried Over	121		134	61	74	46	59	56	40	591	173 3/4		Corry

NOTES: No. 189 Good 2nd choice is BURROWS.

11

NUMBER	NAMES	UNINCORPORATED MEN	INCORPORATED MEN	WOMEN	CHILDREN MALE ABOVE 12 YEARS	MALE BETWEEN 12 & 6 YEARS	MALE UNDER 6 YEARS	FEMALE ABOVE 12 YEARS	FEMALE BETWEEN 12 & 6 YEARS	FEMALE UNDER 6 YEARS	TOTAL	Nᵒ RATIONS PR DAY	FROM WHAT PROVINCE OR COUNTRY	REMARKS
	Brought Forward	121	(c)	134	61	74	46	59	56	40	591	173 1/4		
191	Corry James	1		1	2	1		1			5	1 3/4		
192	Caldwell Robert	1		1		1		1	1	1	6	2 1/2	New York	Farmer
193	Coney³ Samuel			1	1	1	1			1	6	1 1/2	Vermount*	Do
194	Cross John	1		1							2	1/2	Do	
195	Cameron Alexʳ	1		1		1		1	1	1	5	1 3/4	New York	
196	Castle Lemuel			1							1	1		
197	Cook Mary Widow			1							1	1/2		
198	Corbin Nathaniel			1						2	3	1		
199	Derrick Phillip			1	1					2	4	1 1/2		
200	Defoe John Pensʳ			1					1		3*	1		
201	Everts Oliver	1		1							2	1/2		
202	Everts Sylvanus	1									1	1		
203	Edy Daniel			1		2	1				4	1 3/4	New York	Farmer
204	Ferguson Richᵈ Penʳ			1		1			1	1	2	1		
205	Freel Peter Penʳ	1		1			1		2		5	2		
206	Fracer* Donald	1		1			1		1		5	1 1/2		
207	Grant⁴ Widow			1					2		3	1 1/2		
208	Gibson Andrew	1		1			2		1		5	1	New York	Farmer
209	Griffs John	1		1				2	1		5	1 1/2		
210	Hooper John	1		1						2	5	1 1/2		
211	Hough Barnabas			1		2	1		2		9*	2 3/4	New York	Blacksmith
212	Holbert Moses			1		1	2		2		7*	2 1/2	Vermount*	Farmer
213	Hoyt Abraham			1	2	1	2		2		9*	2 1/2		

NOTES: 3.   2nd choice Covey - the 1st letter looks like lower case "G" but not the "Fs" above.
        4.   2nd choice GRONT -
        No. 206 - Fracer, compare with No. 380 - same spelling.

NUMBER	NAMES	UNINCORPORATED MEN	INCORPORATED MEN	WOMEN	CHILDREN MALE ABOVE 12 YEARS	CHILDREN MALE BETWEEN 12 & 6 YEARS	CHILDREN MALE UNDER 6 YEARS	CHILDREN FEMALE ABOVE 12 YEARS	CHILDREN FEMALE BETWEEN 12 & 6 YEARS	CHILDREN FEMALE UNDER 6 YEARS	TOTAL	No RATIONS PR DAY	FROM WHAT PROVINCE OR COUNTRY	REMARKS
214	Havens George	1		1		1					3	1 1/2	New York	Farmer
215	Hindman Samuel	1		1		1			1		4	2 1/4	New York	Do
216	Kenedy* Alexr	1		1	2	2					6	2	Vermount*	Farmer
217	London Assa	1		1	1				1	1	5	2		
218	Lever John	1		1		3	2	1	3		11	1 3/4		
219	McMullen Daniel	1		1		1	1			1	5	1		
220	McKinzie* Collin	1		1	2		1				5	1 1/2	New York	Farmer
221	McIntosh James	1		1							2	2 1/2		
222	Millar Ralph			1			2		2	1	6	1		
223	McBane Widow			1		1					2	1	New York	Taylor
224	McGregor Hugh	1					1			1	3			
225	Morehouse John Penr	1		1							2	1/2	New York	Farmer
226	Marsh William Pensr			1							1	1/2		
227	Linsey Darby	1				1			1		3	2		
228	Lindsey* John					1	1				2	3/4		Naughten
	End fo. 145ᵛ (p. 202)													
	Carried Over	142		167	71	97	62	65	81	56	741	230 1/4		

NOTES:

NUMBER	NAMES	UNINCORPORATED MEN	INCORPORATED MEN	WOMEN	CHILDREN MALE ABOVE 12 YEARS	CHILDREN MALE BETWEEN 12 & 6 YEARS	CHILDREN MALE UNDER 6 YEARS	CHILDREN FEMALE ABOVE 12 YEARS	CHILDREN FEMALE BETWEEN 12 & 6 YEARS	CHILDREN FEMALE UNDER 6 YEARS	TOTAL	Nᵒ RATIONS PR DAY	FROM WHAT PROVINCE OR COUNTRY	REMARKS
	Brought Forward	142	(c)	167	71	97	62	65	81	56	741	230 1/4		
229	Naughten Andrew Penr.	1		1	1			1	1		1	1/2		
230	Mabees John			1			1				1	3	1/2		
231	Pettit Dunham*			1	2		1			1		4	1		
232	Phyler Samuel			1					2			7	2		
233	Pickel John			1								1	1/2		
234	Patterson George			1	1		1	2				1	1/4		
235	Rose Matthias Senr.			1	1							4	1/2		
236	Richardson Saml.			1	2			1				5	1/2		
237	Smyth John Tory	1		1				1			3	1 1/2	New York	Farmer
238	Smyth Benonea*	1		1		1		1				2	1		
239	Sealy Joseph	1		1					1			2	1/2		
240	Smith John	1		1			1					3	1/4	New York	
241	Simpson Robert	1		1					1		2	1/2	Vermount*	Carpenter
242	Smith Samuel	1		1						1		1	1/2	Do	Armorer
243	Smith Comfort			1		2	2	1		1	8	2 1/4		
244	Spooner Ralph	1		1		2	1				4	1 3/4		
245	Tuttle Widow			1		1		1			3	1 1/4		
246	Tichont William	1		1		1				1	4	1 1/4	New York	
247	Thos James			1				1	3	1	6	2 1/4		
248	Thompson Jacob			1	2	3		2		1	8	1 1/2		
249	Wraff Richard	1		1				1	1	1	3	1 1/4	New York	Blacksmith
250	Watson Ralph			1	1	2		2	2		7	1 1/4	New York	
251	Wright Samuel	1				2		2		1		3 1/4	New York	Farmer

NOTES:

14

NUMBER	NAMES	UNINCORPORATED MEN	INCORPORATED MEN	WOMEN	CHILDREN MALE			CHILDREN FEMALE			TOTAL	No RATIONS PR DAY	FROM WHAT PROVINCE OR COUNTRY	REMARKS
					ABOVE 12 YEARS	BETWEEN 12 & 6 YEARS	UNDER 6 YEARS	ABOVE 12 YEARS	BETWEEN 12 & 6 YEARS	UNDER 6 YEARS				
252	Wright Ebenezer	1		1	1			1	1		4	1 1/2	Do	Do
253	Widow Wood			1			1	1	1		4	1 1/2		
254	Wiltsie Benoni*	1		1		1				1	4	2 1/2	New York	Farmer
255	Waywood Thomas	1		1		1			1	2	4	1 1/2		
256	Welsh Samuel	1		1					1		2			
257	Wehr Christian Lt. 5	1		1		1	1	2	1	2	9	3 1/4	New York	Farmer
258	Young Alexr	1									1	(b)	Do	
259	Anderson John	1									1	(b)	Do	
260	Bothwick Joshua	1									1	(b)	Vermount*	Farmer
261	Burret Stephen6	1									1	(b)	Do	Do
262	Benedick Elijah	1									1	(b)	Do	
263	Burney William	1							1		1	(b)	New York	
264	Bremer George Junr	1					1				1	(b)		
265	Burton Thomas	1									1			
266	Sherwood Thomas			1							3	1 1/4		Beeby
	End fo. 146 (p. 203)													
	Carried Over	160		193	79	113	72	79	97	69	862	270 1/2		

NOTES: 5. 2nd choice Wehn.
6. 2nd choice Barret.

15

NUMBER	NAMES	MEN UNINCORPORATED	INCORPORATED MEN	WOMEN	CHILDREN MALE ABOVE 12 YEARS	MALE BETWEEN 12 & 6 YEARS	MALE UNDER 6 YEARS	FEMALE ABOVE 12 YEARS	FEMALE BETWEEN 12 & 6 YEARS	FEMALE UNDER 6 YEARS	TOTAL	No RATIONS PR DAY	FROM WHAT PROVINCE OR COUNTRY	REMARKS
	Brought Forward	160	(c)	193	79	113	72	79	97	69	862	270 1/2		
267	Beeby Peter	1		1							1	(b)		
268	Busbin Robt 7	1		1						2	4	(b)	New York	Farmer
269	Boyle George	1		2							3	(b)	Do	Do
270	Clawson Caleb	1		1						2	3	(b)	Do	
271	Chambers John	1									1	(b)	Do	
272	Chilton T. Robert	1		1			1				3	(b)		
273	Campbell Duncan	1									1	(b)		
274	Cook Thomas	1									1	(b)		
275	Darrak James	1									1	(b)		
276	Duglass Robt 8	1									1	(b)		
277	Duglas John 8	1									1	(b)		
278	Detlor Petor*	1		1							2	(b)	New York	Farmer
279	Dimon John	1		1							1	(b)	Vermount*	
280	Enets Roswell	1									1	(b)		
281	Griggs Abraham	1		2						1	4	(b)		
282	Gibson Thomas	1		1					1		3	(b)		
283	Gibson John	1		1							2	(b)	New York	
284	Gibson James	1									1	(b)	Do	
285	Henderson Peter	1		1							1	(b)		
286	Huggard John	1									1	(b)		
287	Kenick James	1									1	(b)		
288	Kenedy Angus	1		1			1				4	(b)		
289	Kerby John	1		1		2		1		2	7	(b)	Vermount*	Farmer

NOTES: 7.   2nd choice Brisbin.
            8.   2nd choice Dughass (or Dughas). Misspelling for "Douglas" ?

16

NUMBER	NAMES	UNINCORPORATED MEN	INCORPORATED MEN	WOMEN	CHILDREN MALE ABOVE 12 YEARS	CHILDREN MALE BETWEEN 12 & 6 YEARS	CHILDREN MALE UNDER 6 YEARS	CHILDREN FEMALE ABOVE 12 YEARS	CHILDREN FEMALE BETWEEN 12 & 6 YEARS	CHILDREN FEMALE UNDER 6 YEARS	TOTAL	Nᵒ RATIONS PR DAY	FROM WHAT PROVINCE OR COUNTRY	REMARKS
290	Kilburn Charlus	1		1		1				1	1	(b)	New York	Do
291	Leahy John			1							3	(b)	Do	Do
292	McIntosh Peter	1									1	(b)	Do	Do
293	Moffit William	1									1	(b)	Do	Do
294	McDowal James*	1		1							1	(b)		
295	McKinzie William*	1		1				1		1	2	(b)		
296	McBane Angus*	1		1			2			1	3	(b)	New York	
297	McKenny Peter	1									3	(b)	Do	
298	Miller Gilbert	1		1							1	(b)	Do	
299	McDougal Alexʳ	1		1							3	(b)	Do	
300	Obrey Mary			1	1			1			3	(b)	Do	Baker
301	Overmouth Lacbarah[9]	1									4	(b)	Do	
302	Pickle John 2D[10]	1									1			
303	Richardson John	1									1			
304	Scutt Alexˡˡ[11]	1									1			
305	Sweet Oliver													Stuard*
	End fo. 146ᵛ (p. 204)													
	Carried Over	191		217	80	116	77	82	98	80	941	270 1/2		

NOTES: 9.   2nd choice Onermouth.
10.   Definitely as above (military abbreviation for seconded ?). More likely 2nd Lieutenant. Could also mean second time this name is on the list.
11.   2nd choice SCOTT.
No. 305 no information listed in line beside name.

17

NUMBER	NAMES	UNINCORPORATED MEN	INCORPORATED MEN	WOMEN	CHILDREN — MALE			CHILDREN — FEMALE			TOTAL	No RATIONS PR DAY	FROM WHAT PROVINCE OR COUNTRY	REMARKS
					ABOVE 12 YEARS	BETWEEN 12 & 6 YEARS	UNDER 6 YEARS	ABOVE 12 YEARS	BETWEEN 12 & 6 YEARS	UNDER 6 YEARS				
	Brought Forward	191	(c)	217	80	116	77	82	98	80	941	270 1/2		
306	Stuard William	1		1							2	(b)		
307	Sutherland James	1		1	1					1		(b)		
308	Staat Robt.	1		1			1	1				(b)		
309	Smith Joseph	1		1								(b)		
310	Martin John	1		1								(b)		
311	Taylor Alexr	1		1			1		1			(b)		
312	Towner Athill	1		1	2			1				(b)		
313	Wood John	1		1								(b)		
314	Amsbury William			1		1			1			1 1/4		
315	Brown Andrew			1		2			1			1 3/4		
316	Bonen Luckus*			1					1			2 1/2		
317	Barths Cathrine			1								1/2		
318	Carmen Michael			1	1	1			2			2	New York	Merchant
319	Cameron Alexr 2D [10]			1					1			1/2	Do	Do
320	Chislom William[12]			1								1	Do	Farmer
321	Comer Thomas			1						1		3/4	Do	Do
322	Davis Richard **			1								(b)		
333	Green John			1		3	1			1		2 1/2		
334	Grant Archibald			1			1					3/4		
335	Johnston William	1		1					2			1/2		
336	Jackson James			1			1					1 3/4		
337	Lindsey John 1st [13]			1								1/2		
338	Logan David			1								1/2		

NOTES: 12.   Definitely as above - misspelling of Chisholm ?
       13.   See footnote 10. While these abbreviations could be for 1st or 2nd Lieutenant, they most likely mean the 1st, 2nd or 3rd time a similar name has been on the list.
       No. 316 - see FAMILIES, Vol. 21, No. 1; pp. 50-51. Also see No. 1113.
       ** Erratum - numbers skip from 322 to 333 (323 to 332 missing). This has no effect on index.

fo. 147

NUMBER	NAMES	UNINCORPORATED MEN	INCORPORATED MEN	WOMEN	CHILDREN MALE ABOVE 12 YEARS	CHILDREN MALE BETWEEN 12 & 6 YEARS	CHILDREN MALE UNDER 6 YEARS	CHILDREN FEMALE ABOVE 12 YEARS	CHILDREN FEMALE BETWEEN 12 & 6 YEARS	CHILDREN FEMALE UNDER 6 YEARS	TOTAL	No RATIONS PR DAY	FROM WHAT PROVINCE OR COUNTRY	REMARKS
339	McDonel Kennith*			1							1	1/2		
340	McDonel John			1			1				2	3/4		
341	McLean Mordach			1			1			1	3	1 1/4		
342	Nelson Caleb			1					1		1	1/2		
343	Pitman Russel			1						1	2	3/4		
344	Robins James Lt.			1		3			1	1	6	2 3/4		
345	Scout John			1			1		1		3	1		
346	Spicer Ezekiel			1		2	1	2	1		7	2 1/4		
347	Smith Eliphlet			1				1			1	1/2		
348	Van Camp Simon			1	1	1			2		5	1 1/4		
349	Whitman Robert	1		1	2				1		5	1		
350	Boarder Mrs.			1							1	(b)		
351	Coons Jacob			1							1	(b)		
352	Leahy William Junr			1							1	(b)		
353	Jones Daniel	1						1	1	1	4	(b)	New York	Farmer
354	Ogden John	1									1	(b)	Do	
355	Appelbee William*	1									1	(b)		McNish
	End fo. 147 (p. 205)													
	Carried Over	204		249	87	129	88	87	114	90	1098	299 3/4		

NOTES:

19

fo. 147v

NUMBER	NAMES	UNINCORPORATED MEN	INCORPORATED MEN	WOMEN	CHILDREN — MALE ABOVE 12 YEARS	MALE BETWEEN 12 & 6 YEARS	MALE UNDER 6 YEARS	FEMALE ABOVE 12 YEARS	FEMALE BETWEEN 12 & 6 YEARS	FEMALE UNDER 6 YEARS	TOTAL	Nᵒ RATIONS PR DAY	FROM WHAT PROVINCE OR COUNTRY	REMARKS
	Brought Forward[14]	204	(c)	249	87	129	88	87	114	90	1098	290 3/4		
356	McNish William	1									1	(b)		
357	McNaughton John	1									1	(b)		
358	McMartin John	1									1	(b)		
359	Ross Donald	1									1	(b)		
360	McAllum Peter[15]	1									1	(b)		
361	Jonas Jotmathan[16]	1									1	(b)		
362	Conklin Abram			1			1				2	3/4		
363	Henderson Caleb			1			1		2		4	1 3/4		
364	Harvy David			1		1	1				3	1 1/4		
365	Mynard Henry			1							1	1 1/2		
366	Ridiker Henry			1	1			1		1	6	2 1/4		
367	Sherwood Samuel	1		1	1	3				1	2	3/4		
368	Blakely James			1	1	2	1	2	1	1	9	2 1/4	New York	Farmer
369	Cameron Duncan			1		1			2		6	2 1/4		
370	Carscallion Edwᵈ; Penᵗ			1					1		3	1		
371	Chesher John			1							3	1/2		
372	Ducolen Stephen[17]	1		1	3				1		6	3	Vermount*	
373	Hotkinson John*	1		1	1	2	2	1	1	1	3	1 1/4	New York	Doctor
374	Howard Mathew Pensᵗ			1			1		1	1	7	1 3/4		
375	Smith Robert			1		1	1				5	1 1/4		
376	Little Andrew			1		1	1				5	2 1/4		
377	Brooks Richard	1		1	1	2					3	/4*	New York	Farmer
378	Cameron John	1									1	(b)	Do	Farmer

NOTES: 14. The clerk did not carry over correctly.
15. 2nd choice McCallum.
16. Other choices Jatmathan/Jotmathan et var.
17. 2nd choice Ducolers.

20

NUMBER	NAMES	UNINCORPORATED MEN	INCORPORATED MEN	WOMEN	CHILDREN MALE ABOVE 12 YEARS	MALE BETWEEN 12 & 6 YEARS	MALE UNDER 6 YEARS	FEMALE ABOVE 12 YEARS	FEMALE BETWEEN 12 & 6 YEARS	FEMALE UNDER 6 YEARS	TOTAL	No RATIONS PR DAY	FROM WHAT PROVINCE OR COUNTRY	REMARKS
379	Dimon Jacob	1									1	(b)		
380	Fracer Alexr 18	1					1				2	(b)		
381	Gorden* Robert	1		1			2	1	1	1	7	(b)		
382	Gill Richard	1		1	1		1				4	(b)		
383	Haye William	1		1	1			1		2	6	(b)	New York	Farmer
384	Long James			1							1	(b)		
385	Powers William			1						1	2	(b)		
386	Smith Stephen			1				1			2	(b)		
387	Wait James			1							1	(b)		
388	Hall Benyah*	1									1		Vermount*	
389	Michael Grass Capt.	1		2	2	1		2	1	1	10	2 1/4	New York	Farmer
390	William Atkinson Lt.	1		1							2	1/2	Do	Do
391	Emanuel Alaback Lt.	1									1	(b)	Do	Carpenter
392	Samuel Humberstone Lt.	1		1		2					4	(b)		Potter
393	John Lee	1									1	(b)		Labourer
394	Jacob Shafer	1									1	1		
	End fo. 147ᵛ (p. 206)													
	Carried Over	228		275	100	145	101	95	125	100	1169	326 1/2		jno

NOTES: 18. See No. 206. No doubt as to the writing.

NUMBER	NAMES	UNINCORPORATED MEN	INCORPORATED MEN	WOMEN	CHILDREN MALE ABOVE 12 YEARS	CHILDREN MALE BETWEEN 12 & 6 YEARS	CHILDREN MALE UNDER 6 YEARS	CHILDREN FEMALE ABOVE 12 YEARS	CHILDREN FEMALE BETWEEN 12 & 6 YEARS	CHILDREN FEMALE UNDER 6 YEARS	TOTAL	No RATIONS PR DAY	FROM WHAT PROVINCE OR COUNTRY	REMARKS
	Brought Forward	228	(c)	275	100	145	101	95	125	100	1169	326 1/2		
395	JnO Mosher	1									1	(b)		Farmer
396	James Brady	1									1	(b)		Mason
397	Richard Hall	1									1	(b)		Farmer
398	Robert Conrad	1		1							2	(b)		Do
399	Agustine Pearean	1		1							2	1/2		Mason
400	John Grant	1		1							2	(b)		Carpenter
401	JnS Holmes	1		1							2	1/2		Cordwainer
402	Aron Brewer	1		1							2	1/2		Farmer
403	Elijah Groome	1		1							8	1/2		Do
404	Jesse Armstrong	1		1	1	3		1			9	2 1/4		Cordwainer
405	2) Widow Orser				4	1	2	2		2	1	1 1/4		
406	1) Joseph Groome	1			1						5	(b)		Taylor
407	George Freidtle	1		1							1	1		Carpenter
408	Barnabas Day	1									1	(b)		Farmer
409	John Leaman	1									1	(b)		Do
410	George Harper	1									8	(b)		Do
411	Silas Palmer	1									1	(b)		Do*
412	Widow Wright			1							1	2 1/2		Do
413	Simon Swatt	1					2	1	3	1	8	(b)		Do
414	Michael Taylor	1									1	(b)		Do
415	Carlus Danley	1									1	(b)		Do
416	Ambross Money	1									1	(b)		Butcher
417	Michael Springfield	1									1	(b)		Do

NOTES: Nos. 405 & 406 – no explanation for the digits 2) & 1).

22

fo. 148

NUMBER	NAMES	UNINCORPORATED MEN	INCORPORATED MEN	WOMEN	CHILDREN MALE ABOVE 12 YEARS	MALE BETWEEN 12 & 6 YEARS	MALE UNDER 6 YEARS	FEMALE ABOVE 12 YEARS	FEMALE BETWEEN 12 & 6 YEARS	FEMALE UNDER 6 YEARS	TOTAL	N° RATIONS PR DAY	FROM WHAT PROVINCE OR COUNTRY	REMARKS
418	Peter Ruttin Capt.	1		1	1			1			4	1		Farmer
419	William Ruttin Lt.	1		1	1					2	3	3/4		Do
420	Philip Roblin	1		1		2	1				7	2 1/4		Carpenter
421	Richard Smith	1		1							2	1 1/2		Farmer
422	Mathew Steel	1									1	(b)		Do
423	Jns Dyer	1									1	(b)		Black Smith
424	William Stayge	1							1		1	(b)		Carpenter
425	Owen Rablen*	1		1							2	1/2		Ditto
426	Joseph Allison	1		1							3			Sawyer
427	James Kieff	1		1			1				1	1		Cordwainer
428	Nicholas Paterson Junr.	1		1							3	(b)		Farmer
429	Edward Wilson	1		1							2	3/4		Do
430	John Fitzgerald	1		1		1					2	1 1/2		Do
431	Nicholas Peterson	1		1				2			5	1/2		Do
432	Paul Peterson	1		1					2		2	2 1/4		Do
433	Christopher Peterson	1		1				1	1		2	1/2		Do
434	Abraham Peterson	1		1	1		1				7	1 3/4		Do
435	Mathew Benson	1		1	2		2				7	1 1/2		Black Smith Farmer
	End fo. 148 (p. 207)													
	Carried Over	267		298	111	152	110	103	132	105	1278	350 3/4		David

NOTES: **No. 430** – believed to have settled north of Brockville, Ontario.

fo. 148v

NUMBER	NAMES	UNINCORPORATED MEN	INCORPORATED MEN	WOMEN	CHILDREN MALE ABOVE 12 YEARS	CHILDREN MALE BETWEEN 12 & 6 YEARS	CHILDREN MALE UNDER 6 YEARS	CHILDREN FEMALE ABOVE 12 YEARS	CHILDREN FEMALE BETWEEN 12 & 6 YEARS	CHILDREN FEMALE UNDER 6 YEARS	TOTAL	N° RATIONS PR DAY	FROM WHAT PROVINCE OR COUNTRY	REMARKS
	Brought Forward	267	(c)	298	111	152	110	103	132	105	1278	350 3/4		
436	David Demera	1					1				1	(b)		Farmer
437	Albert Cornwall	1		1		1	1				4	2 1/4		Do
438	JnS Baker	1			1						2	1/2		Do
439	John Bush	1									1	1		Do
440	Isac* Yorks	1		1					1		3	3		Cordwainer
441	John Rykerman	1		1	2	1		2			7	2	New York	Merchant of some property
442	Daniel McGivin Ct.19	1		1						1	4	1 1/4		
443	George Golloway Lt.	1		1			2				3	(b)		Carpenter
444	John Jones	1		1							2	1/2		Tayler*
445	Obediah Stillwill*	1					1				3	(b)		Cordwainer
446	John Chapman	1									1	(b)		Do
447	Michael Dobbs	1						1			2	1/2		Carpenter
448	JnS Carman	1		1			2		1		5	1 1/2		Do
449	John Everit Capn.	1		1			1				3	3/4		Farmer
450	David Purdy Lt.	1									1	(b)		Carpenter
451	Gilbert Purdy	1									1	(b)		Do
452	Mary Ganter	1		1		1	1				4	(b)		Farmer
453	Robert Greyham	1		1		1	1				4	1 1/4		Butcher
454	William Money	1									1	(b)	Philadelphia	White Smith of some property
455	AlexI Smith	1		1			1			1	4	(b)		Taylor
456	James Damsen	1									1	(b)		

NOTES: 19. Definitely Ct vs Lt. of No. 443. Same as "t" of No. 443, very close to the margin with only space for two letters. This abbreviation also occurs at No. 437 above. Thus, it could represent Captain.

NUMBER	NAMES	UNINCORPORATED MEN	INCORPORATED MEN	WOMEN	CHILDREN — MALE ABOVE 12 YEARS	MALE BETWEEN 12 & 6 YEARS	MALE UNDER 6 YEARS	FEMALE ABOVE 12 YEARS	FEMALE BETWEEN 12 & 6 YEARS	FEMALE UNDER 6 YEARS	TOTAL	N° RATIONS PR DAY	FROM WHAT PROVINCE OR COUNTRY	REMARKS
457	Thomas Dorsey Ct.19	1		1				1	1		4	1		
458	Thomas More Lt.	1									1	(b)		Shipwright
459	John Robinson Lt.	1		1	1	1					4	1 1/4		Farmer
460	George Gilker	1		1		1	1		4		8	3 1/2		
461	William Campbell	1		1	1		1				4	1 1/2		Labourer
462	Mordica * Dorn	1									1	(b)		Do
463	Patrick Fore20	1		1							2	(b)		Cordwainer
464	Charlus Grimsley	1		1						1	3	1		Do
465	William Grimsley	1									1	1		Do
466	Andrew Forster	1		1				1		1	4	1		
467	John Cluck	1		1							2	1 1/2		Potter
468	Hugh Brannan21	1									1	(b)		Farmer
469	Joseph Ailsworth22	1									1	(b)		Baker
470	James McDunn	1									1	(b)		Sawyer
471	Stepford Russel	1		1				1			3	(b)		Cordwainer
472	Robert Shaw	1									1	(b)		Do
473	Daniel Lieson*	1									1	(b)		Paper Stainer
474	Joel Readman	1							1		2	1/2		Blacksmith
475	Henry Benter													Do
	End fo. 128ᵛ (p. 208)													William
	Carried Over	306		317	117	158	121	109	140	109	1377	376 1/2		

NOTES:
20. The capital "G" and "F" could be confused if one did not compare the two in various situations. The "F" is like a modern printed "F" with two definite cross-bars. The "G" is like a lower case modern written "F".
21. 2nd choice Braman (poor choice).
22. 2nd choice Allsworth.
No. 475 – no information listed in line beside name.

fo. 149

NUMBER	NAMES	UNINCORPORATED MEN	INCORPORATED MEN	WOMEN	CHILDREN — MALE			CHILDREN — FEMALE			TOTAL	No RATIONS PR DAY	FROM WHAT PROVINCE OR COUNTRY	REMARKS
					ABOVE 12 YEARS	BETWEEN 12 & 6 YEARS	UNDER 6 YEARS	ABOVE 12 YEARS	BETWEEN 12 & 6 YEARS	UNDER 6 YEARS				
	Brought Forward	306	**	317	117	158	121	109	140	109	1377	376 1/2		
476	William Wills	1									1	(b)		Ship Wright
477	John Ferris	1									1	(b)		Farmer
478	Dennis Whorring	1									1	(b)		Carpenter
479	Daniel Smith	1		1		1	1		1	1	5	2 3/4		Painter
480	Abraham Mabie Ct.19	1		1					1	1	4	1 1/4		Farmer
481	Peter Valoe Lt.	1		1	1	2					5	3/4		Do
482	Paul Huff	1		1	1	2					5	2 1/2		Carpenter
483	Thomas Durling	1						1			2	2 1/2		Farmer
484	Peter Delya	1		1	2	1		1			6	2 1/2		Do
485	William Bell	1									1	(b)		Do
486	Gilbert Bogert	1		1				1			3	1/2		Do
487	John Persals	1		1		1					3	3/4		Carpenter
488	Elias Holmes	1		1		2			1		5	2 1/2		Do
489	William Clark	1		1			2				4	1		Do
490	John Perre	1									1	(b)	New York	Freed Negro of good Connections
491	James Gale Captn	1		1							2	1/2		
492	John Waldenbrock	1									1	(b)		Black Smith
493	Samuel Dean Lt.	1		1		2		1			5	1 1/2		Carpenter
494	Moses Dean	1		1							2	1/2		Farmer
495	Benjamin Valentine	1									1	(b)		Do
496	Thomas Burnet	1		1					1		3	1		Do
497	John Burnet	1									1	(b)		Labourer
498	Mathew Burnet	1									1	(b)		Do

NOTES:

26

NUMBER	NAMES	UNINCORPORATED MEN	INCORPORATED MEN	WOMEN	CHILDREN MALE ABOVE 12 YEARS	CHILDREN MALE BETWEEN 12 & 6 YEARS	CHILDREN MALE UNDER 6 YEARS	CHILDREN FEMALE ABOVE 12 YEARS	CHILDREN FEMALE BETWEEN 12 & 6 YEARS	CHILDREN FEMALE UNDER 6 YEARS	TOTAL	No RATIONS PR DAY	FROM WHAT PROVINCE OR COUNTRY	REMARKS
499	William More	1		1						1	3	1		Carpenter
500	Alexr White Capn	1		1							2	1/2	New York	(formerly Sheriff of Tryon County of no property*
501	Benjamin Clintch	1									1	(b)		
502	John Monier	1		1							2	1/2		
503	Nicholas Hagerman	1									1	(b)	Do	
504	Benjamin Galloway	1		2			2		1	4	8	2 3/4	Do	Farmer
505	Antony Wilmott	1		1		1			1	1	7	3/4	Do	Cordwainer
506	William Bennit*	1									1	1/2		Farmer
507	John Thorne	1		1							1	1		a Cripple
508	Fredrick Williams	1		2	1	2		1	2		4	2 1/2		Black Smith
509	Philip Cook	1		1	1	1		1	1		8	3 1/2		Farmer
510	Jacob Dies	1		1					2		7	2 1/4		Carpenter
511	George Seybert	1				1					2	1/2		Do
512	Jelles Bush	1									2	1/2		Tanner
513	Michael Dedrick	1		1	1	2		1			1	(b)		Hatter
514	George Haase	1		1	2	1			1		6	1 1/2		Butcher
515	Christopher Searon	1									6	3		Carpenter
516	Abraham Collard	1									1	(b)		Farmer
	End fo. 149 (p. 209)													
	Carried Over	347		343	127	176	126	116	153	115	1053	418 1/4		M:

1503

NOTES: Total Column – A correction was made in faint writing below the total for the page as a transposition of the figures was made by the clerk. The correction is carried over to page 210.

NUMBER	NAMES	UNINCORPORATED MEN	INCORPORATED MEN	WOMEN	MALE ABOVE 12 YEARS	MALE BETWEEN 12 & 6 YEARS	MALE UNDER 6 YEARS	FEMALE ABOVE 12 YEARS	FEMALE BETWEEN 12 & 6 YEARS	FEMALE UNDER 6 YEARS	TOTAL	Nº RATIONS PR DAY	FROM WHAT PROVINCE OR COUNTRY	REMARKS
	Brought Forward	347	**	343	127	176	126	116	153	115	1053 / 1503	418 1/4		
517	Mʳ Shaw	1		1	2						4	(b)		Inkeeper*
518	Jns Henry Orsing	1		1							2	1 1/2		Docter*
519	Ezekiel Ousterhout	1		1							2	1/2		Wheeler
520	MᴱS Fonya* 23			1							1	(b)		Mason
521	Henry Tillinback	1		1		1	2		1		6	1 3/4		Farmer
522	Jacob Cook	1									1	(b)		Underage
523	Freed Negros	1		1							2	(b)		
524	MᴱS Willᵐ Adams			1			1				2	(b)		
525	MᴱS Brownson			1			1				2	(b)		
526	MᴱS Buck			1	1	2	1	2	1		8	(b)		
527	MᴱS Butler			1	1	2			2	1	7	(b)		
528	MᴱS Bustead			1							1	(b)		
529	MᴱS Brown			1		1			1		3	(b)		
530	Joseph Brown	1		1							2	(b)	New York	Superanuated*
531	Alexʳ Campbell	1		1	1	2			2	2	9	(b)		Farmer
532	MᴱS Curtiss			1	1	1		1	1		5	(b)		
533	Andrew Coulter	1		1	1	2		1	1	1	8	(b)	New York	Farmer
534	MᴱS Carly			1	1						2	(b)		
535	MᴱS Castle			1		1					2	(b)		
536	MᴱS Carmeron*			1							1	(b)		
537	MᴱS Crysodel*			1		1			2	1	5	(b)		
538	Daniel Fracer	1		1	1		2	1	1		7	(b)		
539	MᴱS Friot			1							1	(b)	New York	Farmer

NOTES: 23. Intriguingly close to the name "Fonda" – a famous Mohawk Valley Colonial hero. All of Lot 14, Second Concession of Lake (Lancaster) Township is shown allocated on McNiff's 1786 Map to a TANNS (JAMES ?) FONDA a Negro.

NUMBER	NAMES	UNINCORPORATED MEN	INCORPORATED MEN	WOMEN	CHILDREN MALE ABOVE 12 YEARS	CHILDREN MALE BETWEEN 12 & 6 YEARS	CHILDREN MALE UNDER 6 YEARS	CHILDREN FEMALE ABOVE 12 YEARS	CHILDREN FEMALE BETWEEN 12 & 6 YEARS	CHILDREN FEMALE UNDER 6 YEARS	TOTAL	Nᵒ RATIONS PR DAY	FROM WHAT PROVINCE OR COUNTRY	REMARKS
540	Mrs Gray			1		1				1	3	(b)		
541	Mrs Germain			1			1		2	1	5	(b)		
542	Mrs Hartman			1		1	1	2	2		7	(b)		
543	Mrs Hawley			1				2			3	(b)		
544	Simon Huntington	1		1		1	2		1	1	7	(b)	New York	Farmer
545	Jeremiah Hil(-)ker 24	1		1			2				4	(b)		
546	Mrs Hamlin			1		1			1	1	4	(b)		
549	Mrs Hoffnogle			1		1		1	1	1	5	(b)		
550	Mrs Huffman			1		1	1				3	(b)		
551	Simpson Janne 25	1		1		1			1	1	5	(b)	Vermount*	Farmer
552	Michael Musport 26	1									1	(b)	New York	Wheeler
553	Daniel Lighthart	1			1						2	(b)	Do	Farmer
554	Kenneth McDonel	1		1					1	1	4	(b)	Do	Labourer
555	James McKim	1		1		1			1	1	5	(b)	Do	Taylor
556	John McMartin	1		1							2	(b)		
557	Mrs T. McIntosh			1		2			1	1	5	(b)		Donald
	End fo. 149ᵛ (p. 210)													
	Carried Over	365		379	136	193	141	126	178	132	1650	422		

NOTES: 24. Could be Hilsker/Hiloker/Hiloker. Most likely HILIKER.
               25. 2nd choice James though it ends in an "E".
               26. 2nd choice Murport.

fo. 150

NUMBER	NAMES	UNINCORPORATED MEN	INCORPORATED MEN	WOMEN	CHILDREN MALE ABOVE 12 YEARS	MALE BETWEEN 12 & 6 YEARS	MALE UNDER 6 YEARS	FEMALE ABOVE 12 YEARS	FEMALE BETWEEN 12 & 6 YEARS	FEMALE UNDER 6 YEARS	TOTAL	Nº RATIONS PR DAY	FROM WHAT PROVINCE OR COUNTRY	REMARKS
	Brought Forward	365	**	379	136	193	141	126	178	132	1650	422		
558	Donald McIntosh	1		1	2					1	4	(b)	Vermount*	Farmer
559	Garrit Miller	1		1		1	1		1	2	8	(b)	New York	Do
560	Mrs McNeil			1						1	2	(b)		
561	Widow McPherson			1							1	(b)		
562	Hugh McDonald	1		1		1			2		3	(b)	New York	Labourer
563	Mrs Northrop			1		1		1	3	1	6	(b)	New York	Farmer
564	Samuel Perry	1		1	1		2	2	1		10	(b)		
565	Mrs Phelps			1			2				2	(b)		
566	Mrs Richardson			1	2	3	2	1			8	(b)		
567	Mrs Samuel Rose			1		3				3	9	(b)		
568	Mrs Daniel Rose			1							1	(b)		
569	Jns Low			1							1	(b)		
570	Widow & Mrs Rogers			2	2		2		1		4	(b)		
571	Mrs David Scott			1		1	1	1		1	6	(b)		
572	Mrs Daniel Scott			1			1		1		2	(b)		
573	Mrs Tyler			1	1	1	1		3		4	(b)		
574	Mrs Wilson	1		1	1	1	1				7	(b)	New York	
575	Henry Young			1	1	1			1		3	(b)		
576	Mrs Bull			1	2						3	(b)		
577	Mrs Jones's children										3	(b)		
578	Cathe Chilchrist			1							1	(b)		
579	Jns McDonald										1	(b)		
580	William Armstrong	1					1				1	(b)	New York	Superanuated*

NOTES:

NUMBER	NAMES	UNINCORPORATED MEN	INCORPORATED MEN	WOMEN	CHILDREN — MALE ABOVE 12 YEARS	MALE BETWEEN 12 & 6 YEARS	MALE UNDER 6 YEARS	FEMALE ABOVE 12 YEARS	FEMALE BETWEEN 12 & 6 YEARS	FEMALE UNDER 6 YEARS	TOTAL	Nᵒ RATIONS PR DAY	FROM WHAT PROVINCE OR COUNTRY	REMARKS
581	Andress Stull	1		1	1	1	1		1	1	7	(b)	Do	Farmer
582	Mrs Wm Fracer Capn.			1		1			1		3	(b)		
583	Mrs Thomas Fracer			1		1			1		3	(b)		
584	Mrs Adams Lt.			1				1			2	(b)		
585	Mrs Wm Fracer Senr.			1							1	(b)		
586	Mrs John Fracer			1		2	1				4	(b)	New York	Farmer
587	Mrs Washburn			1							1	(b)		
588	Mrs Ross			1							1	(b)		
589	Mrs Humphry			1			2			1	4	(b)		
590	Mrs R. Mott			1			1				2	(b)		
591	Mrs Snyder			1			1			2	4	(b)		
592	Hufnail John	1		1			2			1	5	(b)		
593	Hufnail Mrs			1							1	(b)		Mrs
	End fo. 150 (p. 211)													
	Carried Over	373		414	148	213	159	132	194	149	1182	422		

NOTES:

NUMBER	NAMES	UNINCORPORATED MEN	INCORPORATED MEN	WOMEN	CHILDREN — MALE ABOVE 12 YEARS	MALE BETWEEN 12 & 6 YEARS	MALE UNDER 6 YEARS	FEMALE ABOVE 12 YEARS	FEMALE BETWEEN 12 & 6 YEARS	FEMALE UNDER 6 YEARS	TOTAL	No RATIONS PR DAY	FROM WHAT PROVINCE OR COUNTRY	REMARKS
	Brought Forward	373	**	414	148	213	159	132	194	149	1182	422		
594	Mrs McKinzie*			1							1	(b)		
595	Mrs Saunders			1		1					3	(b)		
596	Mrs Kingsbury			1					1		3	(b)		
597	Mrs Colbreath			*							3	(b)		
598	John Andrew	1		1							2	(b)	New York	Farmer
599	Mrs Campbell			1						2	3	(b)		
600	Mrs McIntosh			1		1			1	2	3	(b)		
601	Henry Clow	1		1		2			1		2	(b)		Gone to the Colonies
602	Benjimin Portor*	1		1							1	(b)	Vermount*	Farmer
603	Adams Samuel			1							4	1 1/2		
604	Amey Nicholas			1		1	2	1		1	6	3		
605	Brown Abraham			1	1	1	2			1	5	3		
606	Amey Jonas			1		1	1	1	1	1	4	2		
607	Brunson James			1		2	1		1	1	6	3 1/2		
608	Bradie Mrs			1		1		2	3	1	6	2 1/2		
609	Bowman Adam			1		1	3	3		1	10	4 1/2		
610	Bets Benjamin			1	1	1					6	4		
611	Brisco Isaac			1			1	2			4	4		
612	Buck Mrs			1		2		2		1	7	2		
613	Bernheart Mrs			1		1					1	3		
614	Crowder Mrs	1		1					1	1	4	1		Farmer
615	Crowder William	1		1					1		2	2 1/2	Deleware*	Carpenter
616	Cass Jonah			1			2	1		1	6	1 1/2	Vermount*	

NOTES:

32

NUMBER	NAMES	UNINCORPORATED MEN	INCORPORATED MEN	WOMEN	MALE ABOVE 12 YEARS	MALE BETWEEN 12 & 6 YEARS	MALE UNDER 6 YEARS	FEMALE ABOVE 12 YEARS	FEMALE BETWEEN 12 & 6 YEARS	FEMALE UNDER 6 YEARS	TOTAL	N° RATIONS PR DAY	FROM WHAT PROVINCE OR COUNTRY	REMARKS
617	Dixon John	1		1		1			1	2	5	3		
618	Demit Garret			1		1		1	1	2	4	2		
619	England William			1		1			1		6	3 1/2		
620	Eartmay Benjamin 27			1			1				1	1		
621	Franks Mrs			1					1		3	1		
622	Ferrington Stephen			1				2	1		4	2		
623	Ferguson William			1				1			4	2 1/2		
624	Forbush Mrs			1				1			1	1		
625	Glasford John	1		1			1		1		3	2		Cordwainer
626	Glasford James	1		1			1	1		1	4	3		Do
627	Glasford Little	1		1	1	2		1			3	2 1/2		Do
628	Chilchrist Peter	1		1		2	2		2		7	4	New York	Farmer
629	Glasford Mrs			1							7	3 1/2		Hicks
	End fo. 150v (p. 212)													
	Carried Over	384		449	151	235	179	151	213	166	1928	490		

NOTES: 27. 2nd choice Eartmay. Good choice as there are two "Es" at the beginning of name.
No. 628 – GILCHRIST ? – because of alphabetical order ?

33

NUMBER	NAMES	UNINCORPORATED MEN	INCORPORATED MEN	WOMEN	CHILDREN MALE ABOVE 12 YEARS	CHILDREN MALE BETWEEN 12 & 6 YEARS	CHILDREN MALE UNDER 6 YEARS	CHILDREN FEMALE ABOVE 12 YEARS	CHILDREN FEMALE BETWEEN 12 & 6 YEARS	CHILDREN FEMALE UNDER 6 YEARS	TOTAL	N° RATIONS PR DAY	FROM WHAT PROVINCE OR COUNTRY	REMARKS
	Brought Forward	384	**	449	151	235	179	151	213	166	1928	490		
630	Hicks Lewis			1		1	1		3		6	3 1/2		
631	Hawley Jephta			1	2	1			2	1	6	2		
632	Hobson Benjamin			1				1			2	1		
633	Hard Elisha			1		1			1	1	4	3 1/2		
634	Hard Philo			1			1		2	1	5	3		
635	Harris M͞rs			1	1		1			1	4	2 1/2		
636	Johnson James			1		1		1	2	2	7	3 1/2		
637	Kintner George			1		1	1		1	1	6	3		
638	Lampson John			1		1	1		1		5	3		
639	Lane John			1	1		2		2		3	2		
640	Munro Donald			1							2	1		
641	McPherson John			1			1		1		3	2		
642	McGremer M͞rs *			1	1				2		3	2		
643	McDonel John	1		1	1						3	3		
644	McDonel Alex͞r	1		1	3	1		1			6	2		
645	Morrison M͞rs			1	2		1		2		5	3		
646	Monies Capt͞s Children	1								1	2	(b) 4		
647	McDougal Peter			1		1			3		6	1 1/2		
648	McDougal Mary			1			1	2	1	1	2	1 1/2		
649	McDonel Duncan	1		1						1	3	4		
650	McDonel John	1		1	1	3			3	1	8	3 1/2	New York	
651	McLerran* William			1		4				1	7	3 1/2		Farmer
652	Oshokinsey M͞rs			1							6	3 1/2		

NOTES: No. 645 – More likely MORRISSON.

NUMBER	NAMES	UNINCORPORATED MEN	INCORPORATED MEN	WOMEN	CHILDREN MALE ABOVE 12 YEARS	MALE BETWEEN 12 & 6 YEARS	MALE UNDER 6 YEARS	FEMALE ABOVE 12 YEARS	FEMALE BETWEEN 12 & 6 YEARS	FEMALE UNDER 6 YEARS	TOTAL	No RATIONS PR DAY	FROM WHAT PROVINCE OR COUNTRY	REMARKS
653	Parks Nath.l			1	1	1	2	1	1	1	4	1 1/2		
654	Perry Robert			1		1	1		2	1	7	4		
655	Perry William	1		1							4	2 1/2		
656	Pencil Mrs			1		2					1	1		
657	Pencil John			1			2	1			7	3 1/2		
658	Robeson Daniel			1					2	1	4	3	New York	Taylor
659	Reed Mrs			1						2	1	1		
660	Raymond Mrs			1		1		1			2	3 1/2		
661	Rogers William			1		2	1	2	2		7	2 1/2		
662	Shermon Simeon			1			1	1		1	6	2		
663	Stoner Martin			1	1	2	2				4	2 1/2		
664	See James			1	1		1				4	3		
665	Sheror Thomas			1					1	1	6	3		
666	Storms Gilbert			1					2	2	5	1 1/2		
667	Scott Francis			1						1	2			Shorey
	End fo. 151 (p. 213)													
	Carried Over	390		484	166	259	199	161	249	188	2096	584		

NOTES: No. 655 – More likely PARRY.

35

NUMBER	NAMES	UNINCORPORATED MEN	INCORPORATED MEN	WOMEN	CHILDREN — MALE ABOVE 12 YEARS	MALE BETWEEN 12 & 6 YEARS	MALE UNDER 6 YEARS	FEMALE ABOVE 12 YEARS	FEMALE BETWEEN 12 & 6 YEARS	FEMALE UNDER 6 YEARS	TOTAL	Nᵒ RATIONS PR DAY	FROM WHAT PROVINCE OR COUNTRY	REMARKS
	Brought Forward	390	**	484	166	259	199	161	249	188	2096	584		
668	Shorey MIS	1		1		2			1		5	3		
669	Snyder Simon	1		1		1			1		4	2 1/2		
670	Steward David	1		1							2	2		
671	Snyder Jacob	1		1	1	1	1	2	1	2	10	4 1/2	New York	Farmer
672	Tuttle Stephen	1		1				1			3	1 1/2		
673	Williams MIS	1		1	2			1	1		6	2 1/2		
674	Williams John	1		1	3				3		8	2 1/2		
675	Vanderlip Fredrick 28	1		1	2	1	1	2		1	9	*1/2	New York	Farmer
676	Peter Vanalstine Capt.	1		1	2	1	1	1	1		8	(b)	Do	Do formerly Justice of the Peace
677	Jns Huych Lieut.	1		1	1			1	1		5	(b)	Do	Farmer
678	John Clasm 2nd Lt. 29	1		1	1			2	1		6	(b)	Do	Black Smith
679	Daniel Higunier	1		1	1					1	4	(b)	Do	Carpenter
680	John Scherp	1									1	(b)	Do	Taylor
681	Leonard Conine	1		1							2	(b)	Do	Do
682	Henry Graham	1		1				1	1		4	(b)	Do	Do
683	Gashard Hallenbeeke 30	1									1	(b)	Do	Farmer
684	Richard Davies	1		1		2					4	(b)	Do	Do
685	Peter Lampman 31	1		1		1			1		4	(b)	Do	Do
686	John Johnston	1		1	1						3	(b)	Do	Farmer
687	William Eichles	1		1	1				1		4	(b)	Do	Do
688	John Driver	1		1							2	(b)	Do	Do
689	Fredreick Lampman 31	1									1	(b)	Do	Do

NOTES: 28. 2nd choice Vanderlap/Vanderlep.
             29. 2nd choice Clasm.
             30. 2nd choice Gashird/Gasbard HALLEUBEEKE.
             31. A Mohawk Valley name.
             No. 676 – see Nos. 72, 164, 1144 & 1224.

NUMBER	NAMES	UNINCORPORATED MEN	INCORPORATED MEN	WOMEN	CHILDREN MALE ABOVE 12 YEARS	CHILDREN MALE BETWEEN 12 & 6 YEARS	CHILDREN MALE UNDER 6 YEARS	CHILDREN FEMALE ABOVE 12 YEARS	CHILDREN FEMALE BETWEEN 12 & 6 YEARS	CHILDREN FEMALE UNDER 6 YEARS	TOTAL	Nᵒ RATIONS PR DAY	FROM WHAT PROVINCE OR COUNTRY	REMARKS
690	Togem* Huych	1		1							1	(b)	Do	Do
691	Volkert Sprung	1		1				1			3	(b)	Do	Do
692	James Grommel	1				1		1			4	(b)	Do	Do
693	Richard Vanhorn	1		1							1	(b)	Do	Do
694	Joseph Allen	1		2	2		1	2	1	1	9	(b)	Do	Carpenter
695	Peter Vanskrever	1		1		1					4	(b)	Do	Wever*
696	Cornelius Vanhorn	1							1		2	(b)	Do	Farmer
697	Andrew Hittle32	1		1		1					1	(b)	Do	Cordwainer
698	Christopher Germain	1		1	2		2	3	2		4	(b)	Do	Farmer
699	William Piers	1		1	1		1	2	1	1	2	(b)	Do	
700	Richard Collier	1									1	(b)	Do	Do
701	Philip Derland	1		1							1	(b)	Do	Do
702	Daniel Cole	1		1							11	(b)	Do	Do
703	Jns Meloney	1									8	(b)	Do	Do
	End fo. 151ᵛ (p. 214)													
	Carried Over	421		512	186	274	210	181	262	195	2241	601 1/2		George

NOTES: 32. 2nd choice Thittle. Good choice.

37

NUMBER	NAMES	UNINCORPORATED MEN	INCORPORATED MEN	WOMEN	CHILDREN MALE ABOVE 12 YEARS	MALE BETWEEN 12 & 6 YEARS	MALE UNDER 6 YEARS	FEMALE ABOVE 12 YEARS	FEMALE BETWEEN 12 & 6 YEARS	FEMALE UNDER 6 YEARS	TOTAL	N° RATIONS PR DAY	FROM WHAT PROVINCE OR COUNTRY	REMARKS
	Brought Forward	421	**	512	186	274	210	181	262	195	2241	601 1/2		
704	George Smith	1		1							2	(b)	New York	Farmer
705	Richard Dunn	1		1			1				3	(b)	Do	Do
706	James Byrne	1			1	1		1			4	(b)	Do	Butcher
707	John Harney	1									1	(b)	Do	Weaver
708	Joseph Dawn	1			1						1	(b)	Do	Butcher
709	Stephen Delaney Esqr	2		2	3			2		1	10	(b)		Formerly Clerk of the County of Albany
710	Captain Allan McDonell	1		2	3			2			8	(b)		Late of the 84th Regiment
	Patrick Smith Esq. (see No. 188)													
711	Patrick McNeff*33	1		1							2	(b)	New York	Merchant
712	John Graham	1		1		1	1		1	1	6	(b)	Do	Farmer
713	Robert Tungate	1		1	1						3	(b)	New York	Merchant
714	Alexr Hair34	1			2	1		2	1		8	(b)	Do	Do
715	Mathew Buckly	1			1			1			3	(b)	Do	Farmer
716	John McGinnis	1									1	(b)	Do	Do
717	Richard McGinnis	1									1	(b)	Do	Do
718	Ludwick Streight Senr	1		1	1						3	(b)	Do	Do
719	Ludwick Streight Junr	1									1	(b)	Do	Do
720	Jns Cole	1		1	1					1	4	(b)	Do	Do
721	Elias Cole	1									1	(b)	Do	Do

NOTES:
33. Clearly McNeff. Likely misspelling of McNiff. The land surveyor of SD&G Counties.
34. A well known Mohawk Valley name; also spelled Hare. The HAREs served in Butler's Rangers and the Indian Department.
No. 707 – Good 2nd choice is HARVEY.

fo. 152

NUMBER	NAMES	UNINCORPORATED MEN	INCORPORATED MEN	WOMEN	CHILDREN MALE ABOVE 12 YEARS	MALE BETWEEN 12 & 6 YEARS	MALE UNDER 6 YEARS	FEMALE ABOVE 12 YEARS	FEMALE BETWEEN 12 & 6 YEARS	FEMALE UNDER 6 YEARS	TOTAL	Nº RATIONS PR DAY	FROM WHAT PROVINCE OR COUNTRY	REMARKS
722	William McKunn35	1		1				1			3	(b)	Do	Do
723	Conrad Vanduson	1		1				2			4	(b)	Do	Do
724	James Green	1		1	1		1		1		7	(b)	Do	Butcher
725	Burrint Lewis	1									1	(b)	Do	Farmer
726	William Jones	1									1	(b)	Do	Black Smith
727	Gaspard Vanduson	1									1	(b)	Do	Farmer
728	Hannah Harris			1							1	(b)	Do	
729	John Jones	1									1	(b)	Do	Farmer
730	Andrew Turnbull	1									1	(b)	Do	Do
731	John Cole Junr	1									1	(b)	Do	Do
732	Jacob Stenberger	*1									1	(b)	Do	
733	Nancy Normand			1							1	(b)		
734	John Harris	1		1	2	1	1	3	1	1	11	(b)		
	End fo. 152 (p. 215)													
	Carried Over	453		528	202	277	217	197	266	199	2339	601 1/2		Abel

NOTES: 35. 2nd choice McKernn.

NUMBER	NAMES	UNINCORPORATED MEN	INCORPORATED MEN	WOMEN	CHILDREN MALE ABOVE 12 YEARS	CHILDREN MALE BETWEEN 12 & 6 YEARS	CHILDREN MALE UNDER 6 YEARS	CHILDREN FEMALE ABOVE 12 YEARS	CHILDREN FEMALE BETWEEN 12 & 6 YEARS	CHILDREN FEMALE UNDER 6 YEARS	TOTAL	N° RATIONS PR DAY	FROM WHAT PROVINCE OR COUNTRY	REMARKS
	Brought Forward	453	**	528	202	277	217	197	266	199	2339	601 1/2		
735	Abels Mills	1		1		2	1		1	1	7	2		
736	William Leahy	1		1		2	1	2	1		8	2 1/2		
737	Colin McKinzie*	1									1	2 1/4		
738	Jno Andrew	1									1	(b)		
739	James McDonald	1									1	(b)		
740	Widow Boice			1				1			2	(b)		
741	Widow Jones			1							1	1		
742	Henry Clow	1									1	1		
743	Bryan John Revd			1		1	1		1	1	5	1 3/4		
744	Beach John			1		1	1		1		4	1 3/4		
745	Barber Abrahams			1							1	1 1/2		
746	Blakslay John			1		1			1		3	1		
747	Campbell James			1		1			2		4	1 1/2		
748	Chambers James			1			1		1		3	1 1/2		
749	Carr Daniels			1		2	1		1		5	2 1/2		
750	Dulmage John			1		1	1		1		4	1 3/4		
751	Dunham Daniels			1		2	1			1	5	2 1/2		
752	Ferguson John			1			1		1	1	4	1 1/2		
753	Griffin Joseph			1						1	2	1		
754	Harris Richard			1			1				2	3/4		
755	Jones Ephraims			1		2			1		2	3/4		
756	Jacson Henry[36]			1		1	1		2		5	2 1/4		
757	Knap Joseph			1		2	1		1	1	6	2 1/2		

NOTES: 36. 2nd choice Jarson/JASSON. JACKSON ? See index.
No. 746 - More likely BLASKSLEY.

NUMBER	NAMES	UNINCORPORATED MEN	INCORPORATED MEN	WOMEN	CHILDREN MALE ABOVE 12 YEARS	CHILDREN MALE BETWEEN 12 & 6 YEARS	CHILDREN MALE UNDER 6 YEARS	CHILDREN FEMALE ABOVE 12 YEARS	CHILDREN FEMALE BETWEEN 12 & 6 YEARS	CHILDREN FEMALE UNDER 6 YEARS	TOTAL	No RATIONS PR DAY	FROM WHAT PROVINCE OR COUNTRY	REMARKS
758	Kelsey James			1		1			2	1	5	2 1/4		
759	Lestes Thomas			1							1	1/2		
760	McKenny Johns*			1							1	1/2		
761	Miller Jacob			1			1		2		4	2 1/4		
762	O'Neil James			1		1			2	1	5	2		
763	Perrot James			1							1	1/2		
764	Proctor Ephraim			1						1	2	1/2		
765	Sharp Gusbarts			1		1					2	3/4		
766	Simons Tutus			1		1			1	2	5	2		
767	Snyder Williams			1			1		1		2	1		
768	Thompson Mathews			1			1		1		2	3/4		
769	Froom James			1			1			1	3	1 1/4		Trip
	End fo. 152v (p. 216)													
	Carried Over	459		556	202	296	231	200	289	206	2439	646 1/2		

NOTES: fo. 153 blank.

Nos. 767 & 768 – pluralized given names.

41

NUMBER	NAMES	UNINCORPORATED MEN	INCORPORATED MEN	WOMEN	CHILDREN MALE ABOVE 12 YEARS	MALE BETWEEN 12 & 6 YEARS	MALE UNDER 6 YEARS	FEMALE ABOVE 12 YEARS	FEMALE BETWEEN 12 YEARS	FEMALE UNDER 6 YEARS	TOTAL	N° RATIONS PR DAY	FROM WHAT PROVINCE OR COUNTRY	REMARKS
	Brought Forward	459	**	556	202	296	231	200	289	206	2439	646 1/2		
770	Trip Robert			1			1			1	2	3/4		
771	Thomas Peters			1			1			1	3	1		
772	Vent Adam			1		1	2		2	1	6	2 1/2		
773	Weist John			1		1			1		5	2		
774	Walker Daniel			1		1					2	(b)		
775	Daniel Beagle			1		1	1		1		4	(b)		
776	John Still			1							2	(b)		
777	John McArthur			1		1			1		2	(b)		
778	Kenneth Fracer			1							2	(b)		
779	Matthias Rose			1		1	1		1	1	3	(b)		
780	John Botherback			1		1	1		1		5	(b)		
781	John Brooks			1					1	1	3	(b)		
782	Andrew Brown			1		1	1				4	(b)		
783	Duncan McGrigger*			1					1		2	(b)		
784	Andrew Little			1		1	1		1	1	5	(b)		
785	Adam Millar			1		1			1		3	1 1/2		
786	John & Nancy Cameron			1		1		1	1		2	1		
787	Peter Pickle	1				1					6	2 1/4		Major
	End fo. 153ᵛ (p. 217)	460		573	202	308	241	201	302	213	2500	658 1/2		

NOTES: This is the end of the list started on fo. 143 (page 197). The journal continues with fo. 154 (page 218) with a list of KING'S RANGERS. For indexing purposes the numbering sequence continues from No. 801.

42

PART II

Roll of King's Rangers

(believed to be more commonly called

ROGER'S RANGERS)

Folios 154 to 156^V; names No. 801 to 1022

43

NUMBER	NAMES	UNINCORPORATED MEN	INCORPORATED MEN	WOMEN	CHILDREN MALE ABOVE 12 YEARS	CHILDREN MALE BETWEEN 12 & 6 YEARS	CHILDREN MALE UNDER 6 YEARS	CHILDREN FEMALE ABOVE 12 YEARS	CHILDREN FEMALE BETWEEN 12 & 6 YEARS	CHILDREN FEMALE UNDER 6 YEARS	TOTAL	N° RATIONS PR DAY	FROM WHAT PROVINCE OR COUNTRY	REMARKS
	Brought Forward (d)	(e)												
801	Major Rogers		1	1	2			2	1		7	(b)	New York	of good Estate
802	James Brakenridge		1								1	(b)	Do	Farmer
803	Israel Ferguson		1	1							2	(b)	Do	Do
804	William Buill		1								*3	(b)	Do	Do
805	Richard Ferguson		1								1	(b)	Do	Do
806	Farrington Ferguson		1								1	(b)	Do	Do
807	Arra Ferguson		1								1	(b)	Do	Do
808	William Bill		1								1	(b)	Do	Do
809	Liba Philips		1	1				2			4	(b)	Do	Do
810	John Morhouse*		1	1					1		3	(b)	Do	Do
811	Andrew Rickley		1	1		3	1			1	7	(b)	Do	Blacksmith
812	David Palmer		1								1	(b)	Do	Farmer
813	Dogal McDougal		1								1	(b)	Do	Do
814	Libious Wickwire*		1	1	1						3	(b)	Vermount*	Do
815	Samuel Richardson		1								1	(b)	New York	Do
816	Daniel Smith		1								1	(b)	Do	Do
817	Henry Smith		1								1	(b)	Do	Do
818	Sith* Philips		1								1	(b)	Do	Do
819	Benjimin* Oakly		1								1	(b)	Do	Do
820	George Hix		1								1	(b)	Do	Do
821	Yellis Van Vorst		1								1	(b)	Do	Carpenter
822	JNS Hix		1								1	(b)	Do	Farmer
823	Peter Ash		1								1	(b)	Do	Do

NOTES: (d) Note that the clerk kept the previous list totals of Unincorporated Men and their families separate from this list of Incorporated Men and their families of the King's Rangers.

(e) This column appears in the original and is not used throughout. Its position, though, is between Incorporated Men and the column Women except on fo. 156, where it is next to the Name column on fo. 156v it does not appear at all. No. 814 - one authority on Brockville, Ontario, suggests LIVIUS WICKWIRE.

fo. 154

NUMBER	NAMES	UNINCORPORATED MEN	INCORPORATED MEN	WOMEN	CHILDREN MALE ABOVE 12 YEARS	CHILDREN MALE BETWEEN 12 & 6 YEARS	CHILDREN MALE UNDER 6 YEARS	CHILDREN FEMALE ABOVE 12 YEARS	CHILDREN FEMALE BETWEEN 12 & 6 YEARS	CHILDREN FEMALE UNDER 6 YEARS	TOTAL	N° RATIONS PR DAY	FROM WHAT PROVINCE OR COUNTRY	REMARKS
824	Jonathon Fulford		1	1	1	3	1				7	(b)	Masichuchets*	Black Smith
825	Andrew Rush		1	1							1	(b)	Do	Shoe Maker
826	Jns Pickel		1								2	(b)	Do	Farmer
827	Christian Pickel		1								1	(b)	Conecticut 37	Do
828	Rogor* Green		1								1	(b)	Vermount*	Do
829	Solomon Steward		1								1	(b)		
830	Jns Grant		1								1	(b)		
831	Archibald Henderson		1	1	2			1	1	2	8	(b)	Vermount*	Farmer
832	Jns Philips		1		1				1	2	5	(b)	New York	Do
833	Samuel Atlik		1								1	(b)	Do	Do
834	Alinon* Philips		1								1	(b)	Do	Do
835	Asial* Bradshaw		1								1	(b)	Do	Do
836	William Griffin		1								1	(b)	Do	Shoe Maker
837	William Fitsgerald*		1	1	2		1	1			7	(b)	Hallifax*37	Do
838	Jns Miller		1		1		1				3	(b)	N. York	Farmer
839	Jns McAuther*		1				1				1	(b)	Do	Do
840	Charlus McArthur*		1								1	(b)	Do	Shoe Maker
841	James Kemp		1	1	2	1		1	1	1	7	(b)	New York	Do
842	William Robertson		1								1	(b)	Do	Farmer
843	William Leach		1								1	(b)	Do	
844	Daniel Cameron		1	1		2					2	(b)	Do	Weaver
845	Johnal Codner		1								1	(b)	Do	Farmer
846	Samuel Brunson		1								2	(b)	Vermount*	Farmer
847	Joseph Kemp		1								1	(b)	New York	Do
848	James Frost		1								1	(b)	Do	Do
849	Andrew Little		1								1	(b)		
	End fo. 154 (p. 218)													James
	Carried Over		49	12	11	10	4	6	5	7	104			

NOTES: 37. These and other examples of clerk's spellings confirms the oft repeated explanation for the reason for the many and varied spellings of some surnames. See the two spellings of McArthur at No. 839 & 840. No. 808 – is this meant to be BUILL, with it being a misplacement for one of the three persons in No. 804 ? See No. 170 for BUILL. No. 834 – 2nd choice ALISSON.

45

NUMBER	NAMES	UNINCORPORATED MEN	INCORPORATED MEN	WOMEN	CHILDREN MALE ABOVE 12 YEARS	CHILDREN MALE BETWEEN 12 & 6 YEARS	CHILDREN MALE UNDER 6 YEARS	CHILDREN FEMALE ABOVE 12 YEARS	CHILDREN FEMALE BETWEEN 12 & 6 YEARS	CHILDREN FEMALE UNDER 6 YEARS	TOTAL	N° RATIONS PR DAY	FROM WHAT PROVINCE OR COUNTRY	REMARKS
	Brought Forward		49	12	11	10	4	6	5	7	104			
850	James Henderson		1	1				1			3	(b)	Vermount*	Farmer
851	John Cross		1	1		1					3	(b)	Do	Do
852	James Lindsey		1								1	(b)	N. York	Do
853	William Marsh		1								1	(b)	Do	Do
854	Alexander McArthur		1								1	(b)	Do	
855	Benjamin Green		1								1	(b)	Vermount*	Taylor
856	Jacob Pickel 38		1								1	(b)	N. York	Farmer
857	Keneth McPherson		1								1	(b)	Do	Do
858	Davis Hanley		1								1	(b)		
859	Christopher Person		1								1	(b)		
860	William Thompson		1								1	(b)	N. York	Farmer
861	Jns Reynolds		1								1	(b)	Vermount*	Do
862	Philip Orra 39		1								1	(b)	Do	Do
863	Jns Purkins*		1								1	(b)	New York	Taylor
864	James McCay*		1	1			1				3	(b)	Boston	Black Smith
865	Jns Hints		1								1	(b)	N. York	Farmer
866	William Grant		1								1	(b)	Do	
867	Thomas Price		1								1	(b)	N. York	Farmer
868	Arom* Wimp		1								1	(b)	Do	
869	Benjimin Mosher*		1								1	(b)	Vermount*	Farmer
870	Simier* Sturns		1								1	(b)		Do
871	Edward Spencer		1								1	(b)		
872	Jns Nichols		1								1	(b)	S. Carolina	Taylor

NOTES: 38. See No. 827 for a Christian Pickel from "Masichuchets".
39. 2nd choice Oera.

46

NUMBER	NAMES	UNINCORPORATED MEN	INCORPORATED MEN	WOMEN	MALE ABOVE 12 YEARS	MALE BETWEEN 12 & 6 YEARS	MALE UNDER 6 YEARS	FEMALE ABOVE 12 YEARS	FEMALE BETWEEN 12 & 6 YEARS	FEMALE UNDER 6 YEARS	TOTAL	Nᵒ RATIONS PR DAY	FROM WHAT PROVINCE OR COUNTRY	REMARKS
873	Elipholet Smith		1	1							2	(b)	Vermount*	Farmer
874	Jno Clemons		1								1	(b)	New York	Black Smith
875	Israel Leak		1								1	(b)	Vermount*	Farmer
876	Price40 Barsley		1								1	(b)		
877	Comfort Smith		1	1							2	(b)	Vermount*	Shoe Maker
878	Linoss* Ross		1	1		1	1		1	1	6	(b)	Do	Farmer
879	Nathaniel Parks		1								1	(b)	N. York	
880	Jns Bliss		1								1	(b)		
881	Jns Thompson		1	1							2	(b)	Conecticut*	Farmer
882	Jno Kimp		1								1	(b)	N. York	Farmer
883	Lurd Borgham		1	1						1	3	(b)		
884	Tididiah* Lirins		1	1							2	(b)	Vermount*	Do
885	Robert Nichols		1								1	(b)		
886	Ebenezer Patterson		1								1	(b)		
887	Frances Van De Bogart		1								1	(b)		
888	James Lindsey		1								1	(b)		
889	James Adams		1	1		1	1				4	(b)	Do	Do
890	Agariah* Pricthard*		1	1			1			2	5	(b)	New York	Do
891	Solomon Johns		1	1							2	(b)	Conecticut*	Do
892	Caleb Green		1	1							2	(b)	Vermount*	Do
893	Peter Taylor		1	1						1	3	(b)	Do	Do
894	George Campbell		1								1	(b)	Do	Do
895	Levi Barnum		1								1	(b)	N. York	Do
896	James Parks		1								1	(b)	Do	Do
897	Jns Hill		1								1	(b)		
	End fo. 154ᵛ (p. 219)													Joseph
	Carried Over		97	25	11	13	8	7	6	12	179			

NOTES: 40. 2nd choice Trice.
No. 875 – there was a LEAK'S Corps fighting in the Hudson River area. It was incorporated into Roger's Rangers c1781. The name LEAK is common in Yorkshire, England and there is an Anglican Parish of that name there. There are square brackets around the "S" of ISRAEL.

NUMBER	NAMES	UNINCORPORATED MEN	INCORPORATED MEN	WOMEN	CHILDREN MALE ABOVE 12 YEARS	MALE BETWEEN 12 & 6 YEARS	MALE UNDER 6 YEARS	FEMALE ABOVE 12 YEARS	FEMALE BETWEEN 12 & 6 YEARS	FEMALE UNDER 6 YEARS	TOTAL	No RATIONS PR DAY	FROM WHAT PROVINCE OR COUNTRY	REMARKS
	Brought Forward		97	25	11	13	8	7	6	12	179			
898	Joseph Marsh41		1	1			1		2		5	(b)	Vermount*	Farmer
899	Abner Barlow		1								1	(b)	New Hamshire*	Do
900	Squire McCoy*		1								1	(b)	Do	Do
901	Lachs Granger		1								1	(b)	Vermount*	Do
902	William Brown		1								1	(b)	New York	Taylor
903	Richard Anthony		1								1	(b)	Do	Farmer
904	George Cosbey		1								1	(b)	Do	Do
905	Henry Cross		1	1					1	3	6	(b)	Do	Do
906	John Conely		1								1	(b)	Do	Do
907	Jacob Demon Junr		1	1							2	(b)	Do	Armourer
908	William Farres		1	1		1	2		2	1	8	(b)	Hallifax*	Farmer
909	Moses Harlbert		1	1		1	2			1	6	(b)	Vermount*	Do
910	Jns Knapping		1	1	1						3	(b)	Do	Milliorite*42
911	Isaac Ines		1	1				2	1		5	(b)	N. York	Farmer
912	Eliga* Munro		1	1	1						3	(b)	Do	Do
913	Jacob Miller		1	1			1				3	(b)	Do	Do
914	Frances More		1	1					1		3	(b)	Vermount*	Do
915	John Nichols		1								1	(b)	Do	Do
916	Samuel Philo43		1	1			2		3	1	8	(b)	Do	Do
917	George Patterson		1	1							2	(b)	Do	Do
918	Henry Pells		1								1	(b)	New York	Do
919	George Speed		1								1	(b)	Do	Do
920	Christopher Curtis		1								1	(b)	Pensylvania*	Cooper

NOTES: 41. An unusual "M" in Aarsh; same as "M" of McCoy at No. 900. Could be Aarsh.

42. Mill Wright ?

43. 2nd choice Phils. Philo appears to be both a given name and surname. There is the chance that PHILO/PHILS is an abbreviation for PHILIP/PHILIPS.

No. 911 - 2nd choice IVES.

NUMBER	NAMES	UNINCORPORATED MEN	INCORPORATED MEN	WOMEN	CHILDREN MALE ABOVE 12 YEARS	MALE BETWEEN 12 & 6 YEARS	MALE UNDER 6 YEARS	FEMALE ABOVE 12 YEARS	FEMALE BETWEEN 12 & 6 YEARS	FEMALE UNDER 6 YEARS	TOTAL	N° RATIONS PR DAY	FROM WHAT PROVINCE OR COUNTRY	REMARKS
921	Stephen Wakely		1								1	(b)	Vermount*	Farmer
922	Jacob Bush		1								1	(b)	N. York	Do
923	John Carkner		1								1	(b)	Do	Do
924	Andrew Adams		1								1	(b)	Vermount*	Do
925	Nathan Noyes		1								1	(b)	Newhampshire	Do
926	Joseph Brown		1								1	(b)	Vermount*	Do
927	Jothan* Davis		1								1	(b)	N. York	Farmer
928	Martin Davoe		1								1	(b)	Do	Do
929	Conrad Houghman		1								1	(b)	Germany	Farmer
930	Thomas Wardner		1								1	(b)	London	Seaman
931	Joel Adams		1								1	(b)	Vermount*	Farmer
932	William Adams		1	1			1				3	(b)	Do	Do
933	Asa Dibble		1								1	(b)	Do	Do
934	Peter Creller		1								1	(b)	N. York	Farmer
935	Jonathon Pike		1								1	(b)	Conecticut*	Do
936	Levi Warner		1	1			1				3	(b)	Newhampshire	Weaver
	End fo. 155 (p. 220)													
	Carried Over		136	36	13	15	18	9	16	19	262			Brewir

NOTES:

49

NUMBER	NAMES	UNINCORPORATED MEN	INCORPORATED MEN	WOMEN	CHILDREN MALE ABOVE 12 YEARS	MALE BETWEEN 12 & 6 YEARS	MALE UNDER 6 YEARS	FEMALE ABOVE 12 YEARS	FEMALE BETWEEN 12 & 6 YEARS	FEMALE UNDER 6 YEARS	TOTAL	No RATIONS PR DAY	FROM WHAT PROVINCE OR COUNTRY	REMARKS
	Brought Forward		136	36	13	15	18	9	16	19	262			
937	Brewir* Hugh		1								1	(b)	Vermount*	Farmer
938	Charlus Brown		1								1	(b)	Do	Do
939	James Curry		1	1	1	2					5	(b)	Do	Weaver
940	William Carrigan		1								1	(b)	N. York	Farmer
941	Thomas Phils[44]		1								1	(b)	Vermount*	Do
942	Isaac Brisco		1	1	1	2					5	(b)	Do	Farmer
943	Nadab* Esteman		1								1	(b)	Do	Taylor
944	Abel Davis		1								1	(b)	Do	Farmer
945	John Curry		1								1	(b)	Do	Do
946	Daniel Edge		1	1		2	1				5	(b)	Do	Farmer
947	Hrium[45] Chapple		1								1	(b)	Conecticut*	Do
948	Wm. S. Place		1								1	(b)	Vermount*	Farmer ?[46]
949	Jeremiah Rynolds*		1								1	(b)	Do	Shoe Maker
950	Benjimin Spencer		1								1	(b)	Do	Farmer
951	Thomas Spencer		1								1	(b)	Do	Do
952	Jeremiah* Spencer		1	1		3	1	2	2		10	(b)	Conecticut*	Farmer
953	A. Prichard Jun		1								1	(b)	Vermount*	Do
954	Nicholas Sweet		1								1	(b)	Do	Do
955	Peleek* Spencer		1								1	(b)	Do	Do
956	Henry Ruiter		1	1			1		1	2	6	(b)	N. York	
957	William Tylor		1	1			1	1		1	5	(b)	Do	
958	David Breakenridge		1								*1	(b)		
959	Philip Ruiter Jun		1								1	(b)	N. York	

NOTES: 44. Definitely Phils – see note 43.
              45. Definitely Hrium – misspelling for Hirum ?
              46. A large ink blot abscures most of the word; definitely starts "Fa....".

NUMBER	NAMES	UNINCORPORATED MEN	INCORPORATED MEN	WOMEN	CHILDREN						TOTAL	N° RATIONS PR DAY	FROM WHAT PROVINCE OR COUNTRY	REMARKS
					MALE			FEMALE						
					ABOVE 12 YEARS	BETWEEN 12 & 6 YEARS	UNDER 6 YEARS	ABOVE 12 YEARS	BETWEEN 12 & 6 YEARS	UNDER 6 YEARS				
960	Jns Ruiter		1								1	(b)	Do	
961	Duncan Bell		1								1	(b)	Do	
962	Timothy Pringle		1	1		1	1		1	2	7	(b)	Do	
963	Elisha Philips		1								1	(b)	Do	
964	Samuel Caswell[47]		1	1							2	(b)	Do	
965	Abraham Dafoe		1	1					1	1	4	(b)	Do	
966	Cyrenius Park		1	1							2	(b)	Do	
967	Mosses* Williams		1	1							2	(b)	Do	
968	William Morhouse		1								1	(b)	Do	
969	Jns Vanzant[48]		1								1	(b)	Do	
970	John Warner		1								1	(b)	Hamshire	2.1)
971	Jacob Dafoe		1								1	(b)	N. York	) 49
972	Abraham Dafoe		1								1	(b)	Do	4)
973	Gilbert Harus*		1								1	(b)	Do	Fredrick
	End fo. 155v (p. 221)													
	Carried Over		173	47	15	23	22	13	24	25	342			

NOTES: 47. The "S" of Samuel written like a "T". Could be IAMIEL.
48. 2nd choice Vangant.
49. The meaning of the raised numbers in the Remarks column for No. 970 & 972 is unknown.

51

NUMBER	NAMES	UNINCORPORATED MEN	INCORPORATED MEN	WOMEN	CHILDREN MALE ABOVE 12 YEARS	MALE BETWEEN 12 & 6 YEARS	MALE UNDER 6 YEARS	FEMALE ABOVE 12 YEARS	FEMALE BETWEEN 12 & 6 YEARS	FEMALE UNDER 6 YEARS	TOTAL	N° RATIONS PR DAY	FROM WHAT PROVINCE OR COUNTRY	REMARKS
	Brought Forward		173	47	15	23	22	13	24	25	342			
974	Fredrick Calder		1	1		1					3	(b)	N. York	
975	Abraham Lampman50		1								1	(b)	Do	
976	Joseph Harns		1								1	(b)	Do	
977	William Calder		1	1			1				3	(b)	Do	
978	George Whitman		1								1	(b)	Do	
979	Michael Dafoe		1								1	(b)	Do	
980	Daniel Dafoe		1								1	(b)	Do	
981	Cornelius Miller		1								1	(b)	Do	
982	John Miller		1								1	(b)	Do	
983	Levi Warner		1								1	(b)	Hampshire	
984	John Grant		1	1							2	(b)	Do	
985	John Young		1								1	(b)	New York	
986	Jacob Dimon51		1								1	(b)	Do	
987	John Tobarge		1								1	(b)	Canada	
988	Ephraim Bennitt*		1	1	1	1		2	2		8	(b)	Vermount*	
989	Henry Catchapak52		1	1	2			1	1		6	(b)	N. York	
990	Conrad Derrick		1								1	(b)	Do	
991	Philip Derrick		1								1	(b)	Do	
992	John Anthony		1	1			1			1	4	(b)	Do	
993	Thomas Cornwall		1								1	(b)	Do	
994	Joseph Barnhurt		1								1	(b)	Do	
995	Christian Snyder		1								1	(b)	Do	
996	William Pringle		1	1			1		2	2	7	(b)	Do	

NOTES:
50. See No. 689; a well known Mohawk Valley name.
51. 2nd choice Dunon – but there is a dot over the name for an "i".
52. 2nd choice Catchapah.

52

NUMBER	NAMES	UNINCORPORATED MEN	INCORPORATED MEN	WOMEN	MALE ABOVE 12 YEARS	MALE BETWEEN 12 & 6 YEARS	MALE UNDER 6 YEARS	FEMALE ABOVE 12 YEARS	FEMALE BETWEEN 12 & 6 YEARS	FEMALE UNDER 6 YEARS	TOTAL	No RATIONS PR DAY	FROM WHAT PROVINCE OR COUNTRY	REMARKS
997	Mathew Watson		1								1	(b)	Do	
998	Jns Forsbury		1								1	(b)	Do	
999	William High		1								1	(b)	Do	
1000	Johnston Harus*		1								1	(b)	*	
1001	Samuel Brooks		1								1	(b)	Hampshire	
1002	Jonathan Murrison		1								1	(b)	New York	
1003	John McIntosh		1								1	(b)	Do	
1004	Joseph Satterly		1								1	(b)	Do	
1005	Daniel Lucas		1								1	(b)	Do	
1006	Gilbert Harris53		1								1	(b)	Do	
1007	Carper Ostwalt54		1			2				1	4	(b)	Germany	
1008	Charlus Near		1	1							2	(b)	N. York	
1009	Henry Oble55		1	1							2	(b)	Do	
1010	Lawrence McKenzie		1	1							2	(b)	N. York	
1011	William Upton		1								1	(b)	Do	
1012	John Dafoe		1								1	(b)	Do	
1013	Doctor Pringle		1								1	(b)		Joel
	End fo. 156 (p. 222)													
	Carried Over		213	57	18	27	25	16	29	29	414			

NOTES: 53. Compare with No. 1000 & 973.
54. 2nd choice Casper.
55. 2nd choice Able.

53

NUMBER	NAMES	UNINCORPORATED WOMEN	INCORPORATED MEN	CHILDREN	MALE ABOVE 12 YEARS	MALE BETWEEN 12 & 6 YEARS	MALE UNDER 6 YEARS	FEMALE ABOVE 12 YEARS	FEMALE BETWEEN 12 & 6 YEARS	FEMALE UNDER 6 YEARS	TOTAL	No RATIONS PR DAY	FROM WHAT PROVINCE OR COUNTRY	REMARKS
	Brought Forward		213	57	18	27	25	16	29	29	414			
1014	Joel Pringle Senr:		1	1							2	(b)	N. York	
1015	Joseph Pringle		1	1							2	(b)	Do	
1016	Oliver Graham		1								1	(b)	Do	
1017	Conrad Col. Hammer		1								1	(b)	Do	
1018	George Colhammer		1								1	(b)	Do	
1019	Joel Pringle		1	1							2	(b)	Do	
1020	John Martin		1								1	(b)	Do	
1021	Abraham Lampman⁵⁰		1								1	(b)	Do	
1022	Pomps Lassi 56		1								1	(b)	Do	
	Total of Kings Rangers		222	60	18	27	25	16	29	29	426			

(fo. 156ᵛ continues with a Return of 1KRRNY on the lower half of the folio. The transcription of this starts on the next page with No. 1101).

NOTES: 56. 2nd choice Lossi.
Nos. 1017 & 1018 compare Col. Hammer and Colhammer (as written),
No. 996, 1013, 1014, 1015, & 1019 PRINGLE, a well known Cornwall, Ontario Loyalist name.

54

PART III

Return of the 1st Battalion

of the King's Royal Regiment of New York (1KRRNY)

also known as The Royal Yorkers.

Folios 156^v to 162; names No. 1101 to 1560

fo. 156v continued

Return of the 1st Battalⁿ of the Kings Royal Regt. New York

p. 223

NUMBER	NAMES	UNINCORPORATED MEN	INCORPORATED MEN	WOMEN	CHILDREN MALE ABOVE 12 YEARS	MALE BETWEEN 12 & 6 YEARS	MALE UNDER 6 YEARS	FEMALE ABOVE 12 YEARS	FEMALE BETWEEN 12 & 6 YEARS	FEMALE UNDER 6 YEARS	TOTAL	Nᵒ RATIONS PR DAY	FROM WHAT PROVINCE OR COUNTRY	REMARKS
1101	Captain Byrne	(f)	1								1	(f)	New York	
1102	Ensign Smith		1								1		Do	
1103	John Teeple		1	1		1	1		1		5		Do	Shoemaker
1104	John Pescod		1	1		1		1			4		Do	Mason & Farmer
1105	William Russel		1								1		Do	Farmer
1106	Peter Crouse		1	1							2		Do	Do
1107	Adam Baker		1	1		3	1	1			7		Do	Do
1108	Adam Shafer		1								1		Do	Do
1109	James Van Camp		1	1	1	1		1	1		6		Do	Do
1110	Jns Boice		1	1	2	2			1		7		Do	Do
1111	Philip Shafer		1	1	2	2	1		1	1	9		Do	Do
1112	Michael Carman		1	1		1	1	1	1	1	7		Do	Do
1113	Luke Boen*		1	1		2	1		1	1	7		Do	Do
1114	Robt Davis57		1	1			1				*3		Do	Do
1115	Jacob Dorn		1	1							2		Do	Do
1116	Jacob Coon		1	1							2		Do	Do
	End fo. 156ᵛ (p. 223)													
	Carried Over		16	12	5	13	6	4	6	3	65			Conrad

NOTES: (f) These columns do not appear in the original throughout Part III.
57. 2nd choice Ruhᵈ
No. 1113 - See FAMILIES, Vol. 21, No. 1; pp. 50-51. Also see No. 316.

56

NUMBER	NAMES	UNINCORPORATED MEN	INCORPORATED MEN	WOMEN	CHILDREN MALE ABOVE 12 YEARS	CHILDREN MALE BETWEEN 12 & 6 YEARS	CHILDREN MALE UNDER 6 YEARS	CHILDREN FEMALE ABOVE 12 YEARS	CHILDREN FEMALE BETWEEN 12 & 6 YEARS	CHILDREN FEMALE UNDER 6 YEARS	TOTAL	Nº RATIONS PR DAY	FROM WHAT PROVINCE OR COUNTRY	REMARKS
	Brought Forward		16	12	5	13	6	4	6	3	65			
1117	Conrad Snyder		1	1		1					3		New York	Farmer
1118	Martin Algire		1	1							2		Do	Do
1119	Archibald Grant		1	1			1				3		Do	Do
1120	John McKenzie		1	1							2		Do	Do
1121	Peter Ferguson		1	1			1				3		Do	Do
1122	Donald McCay*		1	1	1	2			1	1	7		Do	Do
1123	William Henderson		1	1					1		3		Do	Do
1124	Corpᶦ James Johnson		1								1		Conecticut*	Do
1125	Corpᶦ Obijah Weed		1								1		N. York	Do
1126	Jⁿˢ Markly		1								1		Do	Do
1127	Peter Dop		1								1		Do	Do
1128	Peter Davis		1								1		Do	Do
1129	George Sheets		1								1		Do	Do
1130	Adam Snider		1								1		Do	Do
1131	Fredrick Weaver		1								1		Do	Do
1132	John Wert		1								1		Do	Do
1133	Adam Dop		1								1		Do	Do
1134	John Kilman		1								1		Do	Do
1135	Andrew Dusler		1								1		Do	Do
1136	Jacob Garlow		1								1		Do	Do
1137	Donald McEntire		1								1		Do	Do
1138	Jⁿˢ Hickey		1								1		Do	Do
1139	Henry Ittman		1								1		Do	Do

NOTES: No. 1118 – in other documents this name often spelled ALGUIRE.
            No. 1126 – see 1272, 1286 & 1290.

NUMBER	NAMES	UNINCORPORATED MEN	INCORPORATED MEN	WOMEN	CHILDREN MALE ABOVE 12 YEARS	CHILDREN MALE BETWEEN 12 & 6 YEARS	CHILDREN MALE UNDER 6 YEARS	CHILDREN FEMALE ABOVE 12 YEARS	CHILDREN FEMALE BETWEEN 12 & 6 YEARS	CHILDREN FEMALE UNDER 6 YEARS	TOTAL	No RATIONS PR DAY	FROM WHAT PROVINCE OR COUNTRY	REMARKS
1140	John Cryslor*		1								1		Do	Do
1141	Simon Swarts		1								1		Do	Do
1142	John Weaver		1								1		Do	Taylor
1143	Patrick McDonell		1								1		Do	Farmer
1144	Lanl Vanalstine		1								1		Do	Do
1145	Fredrick Bouch		1								1		Do	Labourer
1146	Edward Gay		1								1		Do	Do
1147	Gerrit Byrns*		1								1		Do	Do
1148	Jns Thompson		1								1		Do	Farmer
1149	David Bouch		1								1		Do	Labourer
1150	Gillis McBain		1								1		Pensylvania*	Leather Dresser
1151	Winard Mitchell		1								1		Vermount*	Farmer
1152	Michael Frallin		1								1		Pensylvania*	Do
1153	Jns Tewhey		1								1		New York	Weaver
1154	Robert Farrington													
1155	Copl Jns Bradshaw													Henry
	End fo. 157 (p. 224)													
	Carried Over		55	18	6	17	8	4	8	4	119			

NOTES: No. 1140 - this is most likely CRYSLER, a famous Loyalist name and the site of the Battle of Crysler's Farm in 1813 (east of Morrisburg, Ontario).
No. 1144 - See Nos. 72, 164, 676, & 1224.

NUMBER	NAMES	UNINCORPORATED MEN	INCORPORATED MEN	WOMEN	MALE ABOVE 12 YEARS	MALE BETWEEN 12 & 6 YEARS	MALE UNDER 6 YEARS	FEMALE ABOVE 12 YEARS	FEMALE BETWEEN 12 & 6 YEARS	FEMALE UNDER 6 YEARS	TOTAL	N° RATIONS PR DAY	FROM WHAT PROVINCE OR COUNTRY	REMARKS
	Brought Forward		55	18	6	17	8	4	8	4	119		N. York	
1156	Henry Strader		1	1						1	3		N. York	Farmer
1157	John Strader		1	1			1				3		Do	Do
1158	Brand Fredrick		1	1							2		Do	Do
1159	Martin Walter		1	1							2		Do	Do
1160	Duncan Murkeson		1	1	1						3		Do	Do
1161	Martin Walliscer		1								1		Do	Do
1162	William Baxter		1								1		Do	Weaver
1163	William Cottom		1								1		Do	Sailor
1164	Johnathan Armstrong		1								1		Do	Farmer
1165	John Shafer		1								1		Do	Labourer
1166	Patrick Murry*		1								1		Do	Farmer
1167	Jeremiah Dorn		1								1		Do	Farmer
1168	David Dorn		1								1		Do	Do
1169	Renold McDonell		1								1		Do	Do
1170	John Shools		1								1		Do	Weaver
1171	Isarel* Husted		1								1		Do	Farmer
1172	Fredrick Nail		1								1		Do	Weaver
1173	George Gollinger		1								1		Do	Farmer
1174	Adam Shafer		1								*-		Do	Do
1175	George Sriver*		1								*-		Do	Do
1176	William Daly		1								1		Do	Butcher
1177	Edward Foster		1								1		Do	Farmer
1178	George Shaver		1								1		Do	Do

NOTES: Nos. 1167 & 1168 - see Nos. 462 & 1115. Jeremiah Dorn was allocated 1st Concession Lot 3E and 10W of the Fifth Township (Matilda) per 1786 map by McNiff.

NUMBER	NAMES	UNINCORPORATED MEN	INCORPORATED MEN	WOMEN	CHILDREN MALE ABOVE 12 YEARS	MALE BETWEEN 12 & 6 YEARS	MALE UNDER 6 YEARS	FEMALE ABOVE 12 YEARS	FEMALE BETWEEN 12 & 6 YEARS	FEMALE UNDER 6 YEARS	TOTAL	No RATIONS PR DAY	FROM WHAT PROVINCE OR COUNTRY	REMARKS
1179	Ludwick Fredrick		1								1		Do	Do
1180	Lucas Fader		1								1		Do	Do
1181	John Saver		1								1		Do	Do
1182	Adam Foster		1								1		Do	Do
1183	Antony Walliscer		1								1		Do	Do
1184	Jacob Shaver		1								1		Do	Do
1185	Peter Browse		1								1		Do	Do
1186	Ener58 Ault		1								1		Do	Do
1187	William Rangier		1								1		Do	Do
1188	Nicholas Miller		1								1		Do	Do
1189	Evern59 Camoran		1								1		Do	Do
1190	Jns Ault		1								1		Do	Gardener
1191	Timothy Obryon*60		1								1		Do	-*
1192	Elisha Anderson		1								1		Do	-*
1193	Ebenezer Anderson		1								1		-*	-*
1194	Major Gray		1	1		1					7		New York	Farmer
1195	Lieut. Jns McKenzie		1					1			1		Do	Do
1196	Ensign Jacob Glen		1	1			3				4		Do	Do
1197	Serjt. Daniel Campbell		1	1		2				2	2		Do	Do
1198	do. Jns McEntire		1	1	1					1	6		Do	Labourer
1199	do. Ferquart McDonel		1											Serjeant
	End fo. 157v (p. 225)													
	Carried Over		99	27	8	20	12	5	8	8	186			

NOTES: 58. 2nd choice Euer/Ever.
   59. 2nd choice Even.
   60. O'Brien ? An example of phonetic spelling.
   No. 1185 - The wife of a descendant, PAULINE BROWSE, is currently a Conservative Member of Parliament - Scarborough Centre.

NUMBER	NAMES	UNINCORPORATED MEN	INCORPORATED MEN	WOMEN	MALE ABOVE 12 YEARS	MALE BETWEEN 12 & 6 YEARS	MALE UNDER 6 YEARS	FEMALE ABOVE 12 YEARS	FEMALE BETWEEN 12 & 6 YEARS	FEMALE UNDER 6 YEARS	TOTAL	No RATIONS PR DAY	FROM WHAT PROVINCE OR COUNTRY	REMARKS
	Brought Forward		99	27	8	20	12	5	8	8	186			
1200	Serjeant McGillis		1	1		2		1			5		New York	Farmer
1201	do McLeod		1	1				3			5		Do	Do
1202	do Livingston		1	1	1						3		Do	Do
1203	Corpl. McGruer		1	1	1				1		4		Do	Do
1204	Corpl. Empey61		1								1		Do	Do
1205	Corpl. McGregger*		1								1		Do	Do
1206	Jacob Sheets		1	1	1						3		Do	Do
1207	John Cameron		1	1	1		1	1			5		Do	Do
1208	William Calder		1	1	2			1			5		Do	Do
1209	Rodrick McDonel		1	1	1						3		Do	Do
1210	Peter Garlow		1	1							2		Do	Do
1211	Donld McDonold*		1	1							2		Do	Do
1212	Peter Grant		1	1			1			1	4		Do	Do
1213	Donld Grant		1	1	2		1	2			7		Do	Do
1214	Donald McDonald Junr		1	1					1		3		Do	Do
1215	Jns McKay		1	1	1		1	2		1	7		Do	Do
1216	William Rose		1	1				1			3		Do	Do
1217	Donald Cambell		1	1			1				3		Do	Do
1218	Andrew Somers		1	1	1			1	2		6		Do	Do
1219	James Cotter		1	1		1		1			4		Do	Do
1220	Petter Finney		1	1	1			2			5		Do	Do
1221	Peter McGrugger62		1	1	1						3		Do	Do
1222	Alexr McDonell		1	1	1			1			4		Do	Do

NOTES: 61. This is JOHANNES F. (FREDERICK ?) EMPEY, 1st born of PHILIP EMPEY Snr. (See No. 1351). He was born 8 June, 1748 per Stone Arabia Trinity Lutheran Church Register; he married CATHARINA (NELLIS ?) and was a farmer and Shoe Maker.
62. A heavy, black "u" is overwritten on a light "e".
No. 1216 should have read GRANT, Finley; he has been inserted at No. 1459 so as not to disturb many pages.

NUMBER	NAMES	UNINCORPORATED MEN	INCORPORATED MEN	WOMEN	CHILDREN MALE ABOVE 12 YEARS	CHILDREN MALE BETWEEN 12 & 6 YEARS	CHILDREN MALE UNDER 6 YEARS	CHILDREN FEMALE ABOVE 12 YEARS	CHILDREN FEMALE BETWEEN 12 & 6 YEARS	CHILDREN FEMALE UNDER 6 YEARS	TOTAL	N° RATIONS PR DAY	FROM WHAT PROVINCE OR COUNTRY	REMARKS
1223	Danal* McLean		1	1	1	2			1	1	7		Do	Do
1224	Isac* Vanalstine		1	1		1	1	2	1		6		Do	Do
1225	John Murchson		1	1		1		1	2		6		Do	Do
1226	Angus McKay		1	1	1		1				4		Do	Do
1227	JNs Braker		1	1	1	1				1	5		Do	Do
1228	George Winter		1	1		1			1		4		Do	Do
1229	Stephen Ferrington		1	1							2		Do	Do
1230	Thomas Ross		1	1				1			2		Do	Do
1231	John McDonell		1	1	1		1	2	1		4		Do	Do
1232	Capt. JNs Munro		1	1		2			1		9		N. York	Do
1233	Ensign Hugh Munro		1							1	1		Do	Do
1234	Serjt. Murdoch McLean		1	1		1	1		1		5		Do	Labourer
1235	do James McDonel		1								1		Do	Farmer
1236	Corpl. Waide		1	1		1			2		1		Do	Mason
1237	Corpl. Thompson		1		1						6		Do	
1238	Corpl. Van allen*		1								1		Do	Black Smith
	End fo. 158 (p. 226)													
	Carried Over		139	58	30	31	21	25	25	14	342			Jno

NOTES: No. 1224 – This spelling occurs frequently throughout these lists. One wonders if it is not a misspelling for another famous Loyalist name VAN ASSELTINE from Mohawk Valley and Canajoharie Creek area. See Nos. 72, 164, 676 and 1144.

NUMBER	NAMES	UNINCORPORATED MEN	INCORPORATED MEN	WOMEN	CHILDREN						TOTAL	Nᵒ RATIONS PR DAY	FROM WHAT PROVINCE OR COUNTRY	REMARKS
					MALE			FEMALE						
					ABOVE 12 YEARS	BETWEEN 12 & 6 YEARS	UNDER 6 YEARS	ABOVE 12 YEARS	BETWEEN 12 & 6 YEARS	UNDER 6 YEARS				
	Brought Forward		139	58	30	31	21	25	25	14	342			
1239	Jⁿˢ Palmer		1								1		Conecticut*	Farmer
1240	William McCormack		1								1		Do	Breeches Maker
1241	Jⁿˢ Glasford		1	1	1				1		4		Do	Farmer
1242	Henry Baker		1								1		N. York	Labourer
1243	James Robinson		1	1							2		Do	Do
1244	Jⁿˢ Benedict		1								1		Conecticut*	Do
1245	David Beverly		1								1		Do	Do
1246	Jⁿˢ Newton		1								1		Do	Do
1247	Jⁿˢ McCarty		1								1		N. York	Do
1248	Dennis Courtney		1								1		Do	Do
1249	William Rose		1								1		Do	Do
1250	George Johnson		1								1		Do	Do
1251	Dougal McVicar		1								1		Conecticut*	Farmer
1252	Gerrit Esling		1								1		N. York	Labourer
1253	Stephen Stenbergh		1								1		Do	Do
1254	Jⁿˢ Davis		1								1		Do	Do
1255	John Mosier		1								1		Do	Farmer
1256	Michael Hanes		1								1		Do	Do
1257	Richard Mandaird		1								1		Do	Do
1258	James Knight		1								1		Do	Do
1259	Richard Smith		1	1							2		Do	Do
1260	Philip Cook		1	1	3						5		Do	Do
1261	James McCue		1	1		2	1				5		Do	Do

NOTES: No. 1253 – likely VON STEINBERG from Albany area.

NUMBER	NAMES	UNINCORPORATED MEN	INCORPORATED MEN	WOMEN	CHILDREN MALE ABOVE 12 YEARS	MALE BETWEEN 12 & 6 YEARS	MALE UNDER 6 YEARS	FEMALE ABOVE 12 YEARS	FEMALE BETWEEN 12 & 6 YEARS	FEMALE UNDER 6 YEARS	TOTAL	N° RATIONS PR DAY	FROM WHAT PROVINCE OR COUNTRY	REMARKS
1262	Jns Bowker		1								1		Do	Cordwainer
1263	Henry Frats		1								1		Do	Farmer
1264	Jns Bishop		1	1		1					3		Do	Carpenter
1265	Jns Helmer		1								1		Do	Farmer
1266	Abraham Hopper		1								1		Do	Do
1267	George Readick		1								1		Do	Do
1268	Christian House		1								1		Do	Do
1269	James Plant		1	1		1				1	4		Do	Destiller of Liquor*
1270	Jns Shafer		1	1		1			2		5		Do	Farmer
1271	George Louchs		1								1		Do	Do
1272	Henry Mercle		1								1		Do	Do
1273	Sefrenius Castleman[70]		1	1	3	3					8		Do	Do
1274	Jns Crouse		1								*3		Do	Do
1275	Michael Mercle		1								1		Do	Do
1276	Conrad Becker		1								1		Do	Do
1277	Jns Murkeson		1	1	2					1	5		Do	Do
1278	David Rilly*		1								1		Do	Farmer & School Master
1279	Adam Castleman[70]		1								1		Do	
1280	Conrad Castleman[70]		1								1		Do	
	End fo. 158ᵛ (p. 227)													
	Carried Over		181	69	39	41	22	25	26	18	418			jno

NOTES: No. 1271 - More likely LOUCKS.
No. 1272 - See Nos. 1126, 1286 & 1290. Marcle was also spelled MARKLE/MERKLEY/MARKLAND. See the Canadian Genealogist: Vol. 2, No. 2; (1980), pp. 87 to 105; and The Loyalist Gazette, Spring 1976, pp. 12 & 13. This HENRY MERKLEY was possibly the HENRY who came from the Schoharie Valley and later became a Militia Major and MIA of Upper Canada.

NUMBER	NAMES	UNINCORPORATED MEN	INCORPORATED MEN	WOMEN	CHILDREN MALE ABOVE 12 YEARS	MALE BETWEEN 12 & 6 YEARS	MALE UNDER 6 YEARS	FEMALE ABOVE 12 YEARS	FEMALE BETWEEN 12 & 6 YEARS	FEMALE UNDER 6 YEARS	TOTAL	N° RATIONS PR DAY	FROM WHAT PROVINCE OR COUNTRY	REMARKS
	Brought Forward		181	69	39	41	22	25	26	18	418			
1281	Jno Ellons		1								1		New England	Farmer
1282	William Castleman70		1								1		New York	Cooper
1283	Henry Runnions		1								1		Do	Farmer
1284	Jacob Heltenbrant		1								1		Do	Do
1285	Jns Finkner		1								1		Do	Do
1286	Henry Merkley		1								1		Do	Do
1287	William McCue63		1								1		Do	Do
1288	Jns Housinger64		1								1		Do	Do
1289	States Segar65		1								1		Do	Do
1290	Fred. Mercly		1								1		Do	Do
1291	Mathias Snettsinger		1								1		Do	Do
1292	Jeremiah Solomon		1								1		Do	Do
1293	Alexr McDonell		1								1		Do	Do
1294	Jacob Stoneburner82		1								1		Do	Do
1295	Jns Matthias		1	1							2		Do	Do
1296	Edward Herrius*		1								1		Do	Do
1297	Jns Plowts		1								1		Do	Do
1298	Alexr McDonel		1								1		Do	Do
1299	Jns Gramer66		1								1		Do	Do
1300	Adam Knane67		1								1		Do	Do
1301	Fredk Ruport		1								1		Do	Do
1302	Jns Knane67		1								1		Do	Do
1303	Richard Castleman*70		1								1		Do	Do

NOTES: 63. 2nd choice McLue (poor second choice).
64. 2nd choice Honsinger
65. 2nd choice Stales.
66. 2nd choice Gremer.
67. 2nd choice Knave - though No. 1302 definitely Knane.
No. 1286 - see Nos. 1126, 1272, 1290; square brackets around 2nd "E" of MERKLEY.

65

NUMBER	NAMES	UNINCORPORATED MEN	INCORPORATED MEN	WOMEN	CHILDREN MALE ABOVE 12 YEARS	MALE BETWEEN 12 & 6 YEARS	MALE UNDER 6 YEARS	FEMALE ABOVE 12 YEARS	FEMALE BETWEEN 12 & 6 YEARS	FEMALE UNDER 6 YEARS	TOTAL	No RATIONS PR DAY	FROM WHAT PROVINCE OR COUNTRY	REMARKS
1304	Jacob Price		1								1		Do	Do
1305	Patrick King		1	1			1·				3		Do	Do
1306	Jns Link		1								1		Do	Do
1307	George Mitchell		1								1		Do	Do
1308	John Shafer		1								1		Do	Do
1309	Jns Helmer		1								1		Do	Do
1310	Jacob Freece		1								1		Do	Do
1311	William Campbell		1								1		Do	Do
1312	Jacob Ross		1								1		Do	Shoe Maker
1313	Jns Knight		1	1			1				3		Do	Farmer
1314	Adam Cline		1								1		Do	Do
1315	Alexr Cameron		1								1		Do	Do
1316	Mathew Link		1								1		Do	Do
1317	Jns Bouck		1								1		Do	Do
1318	Adam Helmer		1								1		Do	Do
	End fo. 159 (p. 229)													
	Carried Over		219	72	39	41	24	25	26	18	461			Richard

NOTES: No. 1314 - In other documents often spelled KLINE.

No. 1306 & 1316 - JOHANNES GOTTFRIED LINK, bp. 10 Apr 1756 at Stone Arabia Trinity Lutheran (SATL) Church and died 1842 per gravestone, married MARIA EMPEY, born 12 Mar 1770, (SATL) youngest child of PHILIP EMPEY Snr. (See Note 74), MARIA was just about disinherited by her father's Will unless she "came to live in this Province". She did per UCLPs - though not for much as the estate amounted to approximately £15 cash; most of PHILIP's children were named as Executors of the Estate but refused to act "for many reasons".

NUMBER	NAMES	UNINCORPORATED MEN	INCORPORATED MEN	WOMEN	CHILDREN MALE ABOVE 12 YEARS	MALE BETWEEN 12 & 6 YEARS	MALE UNDER 6 YEARS	FEMALE ABOVE 12 YEARS	FEMALE BETWEEN 12 & 6 YEARS	FEMALE UNDER 6 YEARS	TOTAL	No RATIONS PR DAY	FROM WHAT PROVINCE OR COUNTRY	REMARKS
	Brought Forward		219	72	39	41	24	25	26	18	461			
1319	Richard Mandeville Sen.r		1	1	1	2					5		N. York	Leather Breeches Maker
1320	John Shell		1	1		2		1	2		7		Do	Farmer
1321	Frdrick* Fox		1	1		1		1	1		5		Do	Do
1322	William Conely		1								1		Do	Sawyer
1323	James Rose		1								1		Do	Farmer
1324	Duncan McKenzie		1								1		Do	Do
1325	Andrew Boice		1								1		Do	Do
1326	Ephraim Putnam		1	1		1			1		4		Do	Do
1327	Henry State		1	1		3			3		8		Do	Do
1328	Frances Ulman		1								1		Do	Blacksmith
1329	Jns McKaughney68		1	1		2			1		5		Do	Farmer
1330	Henry Cahe69		1	1				1		1	3		Do	Do
1331	Henry Huff		1	1	2			1			5		Do	Labourer
1332	Angus Beaten*		1	1		2		1	2		7		Do	Breeches Maker
1333	Michael McMullen		1	1		1	1	1	1		6		Do	Farmer
1334	Jns Merselius		1	1		2	1		2	1	8		Do	Do
1335	Jacob Mercle		1								1		Do	Do
1336	John McDonell		1								1		Do	Do
1337	Jns Marshell*		1	1							6		Pensilvania*	Do
1338	Dennis Sullivan		1								1		Do	Shoemaker
1339	Adam Shades		1	1		2							Do	Do
1340	Adam Huber		1					1					N. York	Do
1341	Rich.d Freeman		1		1								Do	Do

NOTES: 68. 2nd choice McKanghey. 69. 2nd choice Cake (poor 2nd choice). Possibly CANE.

fo. 159v

NUMBER	NAMES	UNINCORPORATED MEN	INCORPORATED MEN	WOMEN	CHILDREN MALE ABOVE 12 YEARS	CHILDREN MALE BETWEEN 12 & 6 YEARS	CHILDREN MALE UNDER 6 YEARS	CHILDREN FEMALE ABOVE 12 YEARS	CHILDREN FEMALE BETWEEN 12 & 6 YEARS	CHILDREN FEMALE UNDER 6 YEARS	TOTAL	Nº RATIONS PR DAY	FROM WHAT PROVINCE OR COUNTRY	REMARKS
1342	Philip Waiter		1	1	1						3		Do	Do
1343	Henry Castleman70		1								1		Do	
1344	Jns Davy		1								1		Do	Wheeler
1345	Capt. Anderson		1	1			2		2		6		Do	
1346	Lieut. McMartin		1								1		Do	
1347	Lieut. McDonell		1								1		Do	
1348	Serjeant Spencer		1								1		Do	Farmer
1349	do Wallace*		1								1		Do	Baker
1350	do Jns Annable		1	1							2		Do	Do
1351	Corpl Philip Empy71		1	1	1						3		Do	Do*
1352	do Jacob Summers		1								1		Do	Do*
1353	do Joseph Case		1								1		Do	Do*71
1354	Cornelius Bulson		1								1		Do	Do*
1355	William Sheets		1								1		Do	Do*
1356	Cornelius Sullivan		1								1		Do	Do*
1357	Alexander McLaughlen		1	1							2		Do	Do*
1358	James Nicholas		1								1		Do	Do*
1359	Richard Proser		1								1		Do	Do*
1360	Corp. Stauts*		1								1		Do	Do*
1361	Peter Ruport		1								1		Do	Do*
	End fo. 159v (p. 229)													
	Carried Over		262	88	45	57	28	31	41	20	572			Bernet

NOTES: 70, PAC. Haldimand Papers: Reel A-746 - M.G. 21 Add Mss. 21818, fol. 243 to 250; NCOS, Drummers etc., 1st Batt. King's RR of NY lists Henry as age 13; William Castleman as 34; Richard 25; Suffrenus 25; Thomas 15; and, Conrad as 12 as of 24 December 1783.
71. See No. 1204. The clerk has made a mistake in "dittoring" the balance of this page as Bakers; Philip Empy was a farmer. PHILIP EMPEY Jnr. (JOHANN PHILIP), was 2nd son of PHILIP Snr. and MARIA ELISABETH BARBARA SCHULTS EMPEY, b. 2 Oct 1749 at Stone Arabia, (SATL) Tryon (Montgomery) County, NY; his wife was ELIZABETH DILLIBACK. He died 15 June, 1835.
No. 1356 - An error of omission; no name.

NUMBER	NAMES	UNINCORPORATED MEN	INCORPORATED MEN	WOMEN	CHILDREN MALE ABOVE 12 YEARS	CHILDREN MALE BETWEEN 12 & 6 YEARS	CHILDREN MALE UNDER 6 YEARS	CHILDREN FEMALE ABOVE 12 YEARS	CHILDREN FEMALE BETWEEN 12 & 6 YEARS	CHILDREN FEMALE UNDER 6 YEARS	TOTAL	Nº RATIONS PR DAY	FROM WHAT PROVINCE OR COUNTRY	REMARKS
	Brought Forward		262	88	45	57	28	31	41	20	572			
1363	Bernet Heart		1								1		New York	Farmer
1364	Jns More		1								1		Do	Do
1365	John Cayser		1								1		Do	Do
1366	Michael Cayser		1								1		Do	Do
1367	Joseph Cryterman		1								1		Do	Do
1368	Jns Hawn		1								1		Do	Do
1369	Harmonus* Hawn		1								1		Do	Do
1370	Michael Vennor		1								1		Do	Do
1371	Fredrick Bouch		1								1		Do	Turner
1372	James Lynch		1								1		Do	Carpenter
1373	Samuel Sutton		1								1		Do	Farmer
1374	James McClougherty*		1								1		Do	Do
1375	Jones Wood*		1								1		Do	Do
1376	Fredrick Rue		1								1		Do	Do
1377	Charlus Johnson		1								1		Do	Do
1378	Jns Craford*		1								1		Do	Labourer
1379	Jns Murphy		1								1		Do	Farmer
1380	Capt. Jns. McDonell		1	1		1		1	1		5		Do	Do
1381	Lieut. Peter Everit		1								1		Do	Do
1382	Serjt. Jns McKie		1	1			1				3		Newhampshire	Do
1383	do Jns Empey72		1	1						1	3		New York	Do & Blacksmith
1384	do Joseph Benedict		1								1		Newhampshire	Do
1385	Corpl. Nicholas Dannis		1								1		N. York	Do

NOTES: 72. Sgt. JOHN W. EMPEY, b. 1751c at Stone Arabia of WILLIAM EMPEY Snr. (b/o PHILIP Snr.) and MARIA MARGARET LAUKS (LOUCKS); married CATHERINE SHEETS, d/o CHRISTIAN SHEETS. A Blacksmith, he continued with the Indian Department until 1796 when he came to Upper Canada. He died between 3 Feb 1816 and 15 Oct 1817 "when his horse jumped off a bridge" per Heir & Devisee Commission of Ontario. (EKF's gt. gt. gt. grandfather).

NUMBER	NAMES	UNINCORPORATED MEN	INCORPORATED MEN	WOMEN	CHILDREN MALE ABOVE 12 YEARS	CHILDREN MALE BETWEEN 12 & 6 YEARS	CHILDREN MALE UNDER 6 YEARS	CHILDREN FEMALE ABOVE 12 YEARS	CHILDREN FEMALE BETWEEN 12 & 6 YEARS	CHILDREN FEMALE UNDER 6 YEARS	TOTAL	No RATIONS PR DAY	FROM WHAT PROVINCE OR COUNTRY	REMARKS
1386	do David Jeacocks*		1	1					1	2	5		Do	Do
1387	drum. Alexr Ross		1								1		Do	Do
1388	do Leanerd* Stoneburner		1								1		Do	Do
1389	Frances Albrant		1								1		Do	Do
1390	John Obryan*		1								1		New Jersey	Do
1391	Frances Putman		1	1							2		New York	Do
1392	Michael Ault		1								1		Do	Do
1393	Michael Gallinger		1							1	1		Do	Do
1394	Phillip* Stata		1		1	1					3		Do	Do
1395	Nicholas Ault		1								1		Do	Do
1396	John Readick		1								1		Do	Do
1397	Conrad Coons		1								1		Do	Do & Weaver
1398	Martin Meddock		1	1					2	2	8		Do	Do & Blacksmith
1399	Jns Storring		1								1			Serjt.
	End fo. 160 (p. 230)													
	Carried Over	299	299	95	46	59	29	32	45	26	631			

NOTES: There are many well known Loyalist names on this page - ROSS, STONEBURNER, ALBRANT, GALLINGER (GOLLINGER), AULT, STATA (STATE), READDICK (REDDICK), COONS (KUHNS) and STORRING (STARRING).

NUMBER	NAMES	UNINCORPORATED MEN	INCORPORATED MEN	WOMEN	CHILDREN MALE ABOVE 12 YEARS	MALE BETWEEN 12 & 6 YEARS	MALE UNDER 6 YEARS	FEMALE ABOVE 12 YEARS	FEMALE BETWEEN 12 & 6 YEARS	FEMALE UNDER 6 YEARS	TOTAL	N° RATIONS PR DAY	FROM WHAT PROVINCE OR COUNTRY	REMARKS
	Brought Forward		299	95	46	59	29	32	45	26	631			
1400	Serjt. John Smith		1								1		New York	Farmer
1401	do Samuel Moss		1								1		Do	Miller
1402	do Randel McDonel		1								1		Do	Farmer
1403	Corpl. Evan Royce		1								1		Boston Goverment*	Do*
1404	do George Johnson		1								1		New York	Do
1405	do Robert Parks		1								1		Do	Do
1406	Drum Elazer Casse		1	1		2				1	6		Do	Do
1407	William McGlaughlin*70		1			1	1		1	1	4		Do	Do
1408	Verner Castleman		1	1		3				2	7		Do	Do
1409	Jacob Waggoner		1	1			1				3		Do	Do
1410	Hendrick Hawn		1					1			2		Do	Do
1411	David McCoune73		1	1		1			1	1	5		Do	Do
1412	Finley Ross		1						1		2		Do	Do
1413	Kenneth McDonel		1	1							2		Do	Do
1414	Philip Empy74		1							*1	2		Do	Do
1415	Hendrick Gallinger		1	1							4		Do	Do
1416	Calep Peck		1	1		1				1	6		Do	Carpenter
1417	Robert Robison*		1			1	2			1	4		Do	Do
1418	William Empy75		1				2				3		Do	Do
1419	William Pothei		1	1					1		5		Do	Farmer
1420	Nathan Parks		1		1				1				Do	Do
1421	George Crytes		1					1					Do	Do

NOTES: 73. 2nd choice McCowne.

74. This is PHILIP EMPEY Snr. His wife, MARIA ELISABETH BARBARA SCHULTS, had died 1779 in Schenectady after harsh treatment by the Colonists. PHILIP Snr. was born c1728 of JOHANNES & ELIZABETH EMPEY/EMICHEN/EMIGEN and had 8 sons & 3 daughters - 6 of his sons served in the 1KRRNY. There is a mistake in this entry for a girl under 6 years of age. This would be MARIA, b. 12 Mar 1770, his last born, aged 13 or 14.

75. There were only two WILLIAM EMPEYs, (1) WILLIAM Snr., b. 29 Apr 1728, for whom there is no other record of military service; he was a farmer. (2) WILLIAM Jnr., b. 18 Jan 1751, s/o PHILIP Snr., and the only EMPEY who was a Carpenter - so this must be he, (Cont'd next page)

NUMBER	NAMES	UNINCORPORATED MEN	INCORPORATED MEN	WOMEN	CHILDREN MALE ABOVE 12 YEARS	MALE BETWEEN 12 & 6 YEARS	MALE UNDER 6 YEARS	FEMALE ABOVE 12 YEARS	FEMALE BETWEEN 12 & 6 YEARS	FEMALE UNDER 6 YEARS	TOTAL	No RATIONS PR DAY	FROM WHAT PROVINCE OR COUNTRY	REMARKS
1422	Stophel Empy[76]		1								1		Do	Do
1423	Michael Quinn		1								1		Do	Do
1424	Jns Quinn		1								1		Do	Do
1425	William Wormwood		1								1		Do	Do
1426	Christopher Gollinger*		1								1		Do	Do
1427	Adam Hartel		1								1		Do	Do
1428	Harmonus Cryterman		1								1		Do	Do
1429	William Baker		1								1		Do	Do
1430	Conrad Baker		1								1		Do	Do
1431	Hendrick Davis		1								1		Do	Do
1432	Hugh McConelly		1								1			Do
	End fo. 160v (p. 231)													
	Carried Over		332	108	47	68	34	34	50	32	705			Peter

NOTES: William Junr. had 5 sons & 1 daughter; two of his sons, JACOB W. - b. 19 June 1776, and, WILLIAM W. - b. 6 Oct 1777 were conceived before he joined the 1KRRNY on 15 Aug 1777 and lived to adulthood. One, PHILIP W. was born in jail at Albany in 1783 while his father was a POW. Thus, this entry, insofar as his sons are concerned, appears incorrect. WILLIAM Jnr. was a Private in the 1KRRNY; he had been an Ensign in the Tryon County Militia in 1775/77.
76. STOPHEL or CHRISTOPHER EMPEY (aka STUFFLE), was the 7th born of PHILIP Snr. (5th son), b. 8 June 1761. A Private in the 1KRRNY he married CHRISTINA SUMERS/SOMERS and died 28 June 1823 age 61/3.

NUMBER	NAMES	UNINCORPORATED MEN	INCORPORATED MEN	WOMEN	CHILDREN MALE ABOVE 12 YEARS	MALE BETWEEN 12 & 6 YEARS	MALE UNDER 6 YEARS	FEMALE ABOVE 12 YEARS	FEMALE BETWEEN 12 & 6 YEARS	FEMALE UNDER 6 YEARS	TOTAL	No RATIONS PR DAY	FROM WHAT PROVINCE OR COUNTRY	REMARKS
	Brought Forward		332	108	47	68	34	34	50	32	705			
1433	Peter Loucks		1								1		New York	Farmer
1434	Jns Mullen		1								1		Do	Do
1435	Daniel McGilles		1								1		Do	Do
1436	Abraham Freese		1								1		Do	Do
1437	Conrad Davoe		1								1		Newhampshire	Do
1438	Nicholas Matice		1	1							2		New York	Do
1439	Casper Coons		1	1							2		Do	Do
1440	David Catchein		1								1		Deleware*	Do
1441	Adam Empy77		1								1		New York	Do
1442	John Bangle		1								1		Do	Do
1443	John Foster		1								1		Do	Do
1444	Joseph Mott		1								1		Do	Do
1445	Christian Hanes78		1								1		Do	Do
1446	Jacob Sheets		1								1		Do	Do
1447	Daniel Mordin		1								1		Do	Do
1448	Richd Langden		1								1		Do	Schoolmaster
1449	James Wallis		1								1		Do	Farmer
1450	John Paddock79		1								1		Do	Do
1451	Bellshazzer Tellebock80		1								1		Do	Do
1452	Jeremiah Snyder		1								1		Do	Do
1453	Jacob Asten		1	1			1				3		Do	Do
1454	Solomon Tuttle		1								1		Do	Do
1455	Angus Grant		1	1	1	2	1		1	1	8		Do	Do

NOTES: 77. ADAM EMPEY, s/o WILLIAM Snr., b. 1759c. A Private in the 1KRRNY. (The other ADAM EMPEY was s/o Philip Snr, and was a Sergeant). He married MARGARET VON STEINBERG 8 Dec 1803 and died 3 Apr 1824 aged 64 1/2.
78. CHRISTIAN HANES was h/o MARIA CATHARINA EMPEY, d/o WILLIAM Snr. and was b. 30 July 1761.
79. Not all the Loyalists took up land as assigned to them; some returned to the States. A JOHN PADDOCK was assigned W 1/2 Lot No. 33 in Concession II of Osnabruck Township and was claimed by John John S. Empey in an Heir & Devisee Commission Petition dated 10 July 1840 at Toronto (Parcel 61 d/ 1840 John Empey). JOHN JOHN S. EMPEY was the eldest s/o Sgt. JOHN W. EMPEY.

73

NUMBER	NAMES	UNINCORPORATED MEN	INCORPORATED MEN	WOMEN	CHILDREN MALE ABOVE 12 YEARS	MALE BETWEEN 12 & 6 YEARS	MALE UNDER 6 YEARS	FEMALE ABOVE 12 YEARS	FEMALE BETWEEN 12 & 6 YEARS	FEMALE UNDER 6 YEARS	TOTAL	N° RATIONS PR DAY	FROM WHAT PROVINCE OR COUNTRY	REMARKS
1456	Jns McDonell		1	1			1				3		Do	Do
1457	Marchus* Shaver		1								1		Do	Do
1458	Jns Crabtree		1								1		Do	Do
1460	George Murry*		1								1		Pensylvania*	Do
1461	Alexr McDonel		1	1							2		New York	Do
1462	Joseph Loucks		1								1		Do	Do
1463	Jacob Dinney		1								1		Do	Do
1464	William Urquhart		1	1		1	1		2		6		Do	Do
1465	Nicholas Frymire		1	1		1					3		Do	Do
1466	Philip Frymire		1								1		Do	Do
1467	Jns Coons		1								1		Do	Do
	End fo. 161 (p. 232)													
	Inserted as an omission													
1459	Finley GRANT (Proper placement is after No. 1215)		1	1	1			1			4		Do	Do
	Carried Over		366	116	48	72	38	34	53	33	760			James

NOTES: 80. 2nd choice Bellshazzer.

74

NUMBER	NAMES	UNINCORPORATED MEN	INCORPORATED MEN	WOMEN	CHILDREN MALE ABOVE 12 YEARS	MALE BETWEEN 12 & 6 YEARS	MALE UNDER 6 YEARS	FEMALE ABOVE 12 YEARS	FEMALE BETWEEN 12 & 6 YEARS	FEMALE UNDER 6 YEARS	TOTAL	N° RATIONS PR DAY	FROM WHAT PROVINCE OR COUNTRY	REMARKS
	Brought Forward		366	116	48	72	38	34	53	33	760			
1468	James Dingwell		1								1		New York	Farmer
1469	Duncan McEntire*		1								1		Do	Do
1470	Serjt. James Perrigo		1								1		Boston Goverment*	Do & Blacksmith
1471	do James Jones		1								1		(blank)	(blank)
1472	do James Clark		1	1			1				3		N. York	Farmer
1473	Corpl. Jacob Countryman		1								1		Do	Do
1474	do Jacob Criterman		1								1		Do	Do
1475	do John Pratt		1								1		Do	Do
1476	Thomas Castleman[81]		1								1		Do	Do
1477	Jns Stenebrander[82]		1								1		Do	Taylor
1478	Jns Hoopole		1								1		Do	Farmer
1479	Jns McDonell		1								1		Do	Do
1480	Mathew Gibson		1								1		Do	Do
1481	Conrad Wert		1								1		Do	Do
1482	Andrew Wert		1								1		Do	Do
1483	James Mordin		1								1		Do	Do
1484	Peter Carhomhorn		1								1		(blank)	(blank)
1485	Hank* Albrant		1								1		New York	Farmer
1486	Jns Amon		1								1		Do	Do
1487	Richard Hoop		1								1		(blank)	(blank)
1488	Frances Cole		1								1		New York	Farmer
1489	Samuel Street		1								1		Do	Do

NOTES: 81. See note No. 70.
82. A name similar to this is often spelled Stoneburner/Steinburner in other records.
No. 1470 – definitely PERRIGO.

75

NUMBER	NAMES	UNINCORPORATED MEN	INCORPORATED MEN	WOMEN	CHILDREN MALE ABOVE 12 YEARS	MALE BETWEEN 12 & 6 YEARS	MALE UNDER 6 YEARS	FEMALE ABOVE 12 YEARS	FEMALE BETWEEN 12 & 6 YEARS	FEMALE UNDER 6 YEARS	TOTAL	No RATIONS PR DAY	FROM WHAT PROVINCE OR COUNTRY	REMARKS
1490	Barnt Papest		1								1		Do	Do
1491	James Lynch		1								1		Do	Do
1492	Hank Haning		1								1		Do	Do
1493	Jns Dingwell		1	1					2		4		Do	Do
1494	Jns Finnel		1	1					2		4		Do	Do
1495	John Hails		1								1		Do	Do
1496	Richd Cearey[83]		1								1		Do	Do
1497	Michael Whaling		1								1		Do	Do
1498	Hendrick Hoople		1								1		Do	
1500	Joseph Fitchet		1								1			Taylor
1501	Philip Cline[84]		1								1			Farmer
1502	Stophel Service[85]		1								1			Do
	End fo. 161v (p. 233)													
	Carried Over		400	119	48	72	39	34	57	33	802			Jno

NOTES: 83. 2nd choice Ceerey/Cearcy.
84. In other documents this name often spelled Kline.
85. In other documents this name often spelled Servos. Stophel is a nickname for Christopher.
No. 1495 - 2nd choice HAILS.

NUMBER	NAMES	UNINCORPORATED MEN	INCORPORATED MEN	WOMEN	CHILDREN MALE ABOVE 12 YEARS	CHILDREN MALE BETWEEN 12 & 6 YEARS	CHILDREN MALE UNDER 6 YEARS	CHILDREN FEMALE ABOVE 12 YEARS	CHILDREN FEMALE BETWEEN 12 & 6 YEARS	CHILDREN FEMALE UNDER 6 YEARS	TOTAL	No RATIONS PR DAY	FROM WHAT PROVINCE OR COUNTRY	REMARKS
	Brought Forward		400	119	48	72	39	34	57	33	802			
1503	Jns Cadman Senr		1								1		New York	Farmer
1504	Jns Cadman Junr		1								1		Do	Do
1505	Evan Royce		1								1		Do	Do
1506	Samuel Ranalds*		1								1		Do	Do
1507	John Craford*		1								1		Do	Do
1508	Eward* Mann86		1								1		Do	Do
1509	William Dougherty		1								1		Do	Do
1510	George Smith		1								1		Do	Do
1511	Petter* Coss*		1								1		(blank)	(blank)
1512	Jns Gardner		1								1		New York	Farmer
1513	Jns Sawyer		1								1		Do	Do
1514	William Grant		1								1		Do	Do
1515	Jacob Aman		1								1		Do	Do
1516	Philip Gray		1								1		Do	Do
1517	Henry Semore		1								1		(blank)	Sailor
1518	Capt. Alexr McDonnel		1	1				1			3		N. York	Farmer
1519	Ensign Jns Valentine		1	1				1			3		Do	Labourer
1520	Serjt Robt. Gorden*		1	1					1		3		Do	Inn Keeper
1521	do Murdock McPherson		1	1		1	1		1		5		Do	Farmer
1522	do Duncan McCarty		1	1					1	1	4		Do	Do
1523	Corpl. Donald McDonel		1	1	1	1	1				5		Do	Labourer
1524	Jns McNaughton		1		1				1		3		Do	Do
1525	Jns Frazer87		1	1			1		1	1	5		Do	Weaver

NOTES: 86.   2nd choice Marm.
         87.   The "Z" is overwritten with an "S".

fo. 162

NUMBER	NAMES	UNINCORPORATED MEN	INCORPORATED MEN	WOMEN	CHILDREN MALE ABOVE 12 YEARS	MALE BETWEEN 12 & 6 YEARS	MALE UNDER 6 YEARS	FEMALE ABOVE 12 YEARS	FEMALE BETWEEN 12 & 6 YEARS	FEMALE UNDER 6 YEARS	TOTAL	N° RATIONS PR DAY	FROM WHAT PROVINCE OR COUNTRY	REMARKS
	End fo. 162 (p. 234)													
	(fo. 162 only 3/4 full).													
	Carried Over		423	127	48	75	41	37	61	36	848			Alexʳ.

NOTES:

NUMBER	NAMES	UNINCORPORATED MEN	INCORPORATED MEN	WOMEN	MALE ABOVE 12 YEARS	MALE BETWEEN 12 & 6 YEARS	MALE UNDER 6 YEARS	FEMALE ABOVE 12 YEARS	FEMALE BETWEEN 12 & 6 YEARS	FEMALE UNDER 6 YEARS	TOTAL	N° RATIONS PR DAY	FROM WHAT PROVINCE OR COUNTRY	REMARKS
	Brought Forward		423	127	48	75	41	37	61	36	848			
1526	Alexr Chisholm*		1	1		2			1	2	7		New York	Farmer
1527	Alexr McPherson		1	1		1	1		1	1	5		Do	Do
1528	Donald Grant		1	1		1					4		Do	Do
1529	Allan McDonel		1	1	1						5		Do	Do
1530	Allan Grant		1	1		1					3		Do	Do
1531	William Chislom*		1	1				2	1	1	3		Do	Do
1532	James Crouder88		1	1		1			1		5		Do	Do
1533	Adam Bouck		1	1	1	1	1		2		6		Do	Do
1534	Alexr Ferguson		1	1	1	1			2	1	8		Do	Do
1535	Donald McGilles		1	1	3		1		2		4		Do	Do
1536	Donald McCarter		1	1	1	1			2		8		Do	Do
1537	Hugh McCay*		1	1	1			1			3		Do	Do
1538	Jns Duer*		1	1				1			3		Do	Do
1539	Alexr Cameron		1	1						1	4		Do	Do
1540	Donald Ross		1	1						1	3		Do	Do
1541	John Cameron		1	1		1					5		Do	Do
1542	Adam Bangle		1	1					2		3		Do	Do
1543	Hugh McLearon*		1	1							2		Do	Do
1544	Corpl Jos. Stoneburner82		1	1										
1545	Corpl. Alexr McDonel		1	1							1		Do	Do
1546	Donald McNaughten		1	1							1		Do	Do
1547	Donald McDonel Senr		1	1							1		Do	Do

NOTES: 88. 2nd choice Cronder.

79

NUMBER	NAMES	UNINCORPORATED MEN	INCORPORATED MEN	WOMEN	CHILDREN MALE ABOVE 12 YEARS	CHILDREN MALE BETWEEN 12 & 6 YEARS	CHILDREN MALE UNDER 6 YEARS	CHILDREN FEMALE ABOVE 12 YEARS	CHILDREN FEMALE BETWEEN 12 & 6 YEARS	CHILDREN FEMALE UNDER 6 YEARS	TOTAL	No RATIONS PR DAY	FROM WHAT PROVINCE OR COUNTRY	REMARKS
1548	Donald McDonell* Junr		1	1			1			1	4		Do	Do
1549	William Franks		1	1							1		Do	Do
1550	Frances Clark		1								1		Do	Do
1551	George Wort		1								1		Do	Do
1552	Hugh McDonell		1								2		Do	Do
1553	William Bangell		1								1		Do	Do
1554	Henry Bangell		1								1		Do	Do
1555	Peter Bangell		1								1		Do	Do
1556	Jns Hartle		1								1		Do	Do
1557	Isaac Crouder		1								1		Do	Do
1558	Alexr McDonell		1								1			Do
1559	Donald McDonell		1								1			
1560	Jns Wood		1								1			
	End fo. 162v (p. 235)													
	Total 1st Bn Rl Yorkers		458	146	56	85	45	41	83	44		958			Lieut.

NOTES:

80

PART IV

Return of Loyal Rangers – Company of Pensioners

(More commonly called JESSUP'S RANGERS)

Folios 163 to 170^V; names No. 1601 to 2203

NOTE:

In the REMARKS COLUMN the words "Land" and
"Lands" appear frequently. They have been
reproduced as faithfully as possible in case
there is a significance. Similarly with the
words "Lease" and "Leased".

NUMBER	NAMES	INCORPORATED MEN	FROM WHAT PROVINCE OR COUNTRY	REMARKS
1601	Lieut. Col^S Ebenez^r Jeseep*	1	New York	Justice of the Peace Lands & Property
1602	Guisbert Sharp	1	Do	Farmer. Own Lands of good Estate
1603	Conrad Best	1	Do	do
1604	John Stevenson	1	Do	Merchant Houses & Property
1605	Isaac Mann Senr	1	Do	Formerly Justice of Quorum*
1606	John Van Allen	1	Do	Justice of the Peace Houses & Property
1607	William Falkner	1	Do	
1608	William Marsh	1	Vermount*	Justice of the Peace Own Lands
1609	Hugh Munro	1	New York	Trader of good Estate
1610	Richard Cartwright	1	Do	Inn Keeper
1611	Isptah* Hawley	1	Vermount*	Farmer Own Lands
1612	Revern^d John Bryant	1	Do	Clergiman* of good Estate
1613	Thomas Robertson	1	New York	Farmer Own Lands
1614	Daniel Munro	1	Do	do do
1615	Benjimin Hobson	1	Vermount*	Schoolmaster
1616	Frances Hogle	1	New York	Farmer
1617	Joseph Jeseph*	1	Do	Formerly appointed Justice of the Peace own Lands
1618	J^{ns} Mann	1	Do	
1619	James O Neill*	1	Vermount*	Farmer Leased Lands
1620	Philo Hulibert^{89}	1	New York	do Own Lands
1621	Isaac Mann Junr	1	Do	Trader
1622	Titus Simons	1	Do	Deputy Sherrif Own Lands of good Estate
1623	Edward Carscalion*	1	Do	Farmer Own Lands
1624	William Snyder	1	Do	do Leased Lands
1625	James Campbell	1	Do	do of good Estate
1626	Duncan Cameron	1	Do	do
1627	Daniel Fracer	1	Do	do
1628	Jacob Miller	1	Do	do Own Lands
1629	J^{ns} Wilson	1	Do	do do
1630	J^{ns} Lampson	1	Do	do
1631	Josiah Case	1	Vermount*	do Own Lands
1632	Stephen Tuttle	1	New York	Justice of the Peace Own Lands
1633	William Schamorhorn^{90}	1	Do	Farmer
1634	Harmonus Flock	1	Do	do Own Lands
1635	J^{ns} Defoe	1	Do	do
1636	J^{ns} Lampman^{31}	1	Do	do
1637	Simon T. Cole	1	Do	do
	End fo. 163 (p. 236)			
	Carried Over	37		Andrew

NOTES: 89. 2nd choice PHILS; this could be an abbreviation for PHILIP.
90. 2nd choice Schamoshorn - an "r" is written over an "s".
No. 1601 - Most history references spell this name as "JESSUP".
No. 1617 - JESEEP/JESSUP ?
No. 1635 - see Nos. 965, 971, 979, 980, 1012 & 1437 for more DEFOEs et var. This name is supposedly from the Huguenot DEVEAUX/DEVAUX. See NYG&B RECORD 114: 91-98 for other references to this name.

NUMBER	NAMES	INCORPORATED MEN	FROM WHAT PROVINCE OR COUNTRY	REMARKS
	Brought Forward	37		
1638	Andrew Norton	1	New York	Farmer Own Lands
1639	Allen McDonald	1	do	do
1640	Peter Freel	1	do	Inn Keeper
1641	Jⁿˢ Platt	1	do	Blacksmith
1642	James Bradshaw	1	do	Farmer Own Lands
1643	Jⁿˢ Rogers	1	do	do
1644	Jⁿˢ Fracer	1	do	do Leased Lands
1645	Wᵐ Fracer	1	do	do do
1646	David Castwell*	1	Vermount*	do Own Lands of good Estate
1647	Samuel Rose	1	do	do do
1648	George Fincle	1	New York	do Leas* Lands of good Estate
1649	William Fairfield	1	Vermount*	do Own Lands
1650	John McPherson	1	N. York	do do of good Estate
1651	Henry Mattice	1	do	do do
1652	Rodger Stevens	1	Vermount*	do do
1653	Rubin Hanly	1	do	do do of good Estate
1654	Richᵈ Ferguson	1	N. York	Lease Lands*
1655	Mathew Howard	1	do	do)
1656	Reynold McDonel	1	do	do)
1657	Benjamin Hough	1	do	do) 91
1658	Isac* Freote	1	do	do)
1659	Asa Richardson	1	do	do)
1660	Simon Covel	1	do	do Own Lands
1661	Reverand* Mʳ Gilman	1	do	Cergyman*
1662	Major Edward Jeseep[92]	1	do	Justice of the Peace Own Lands
1663	Lieut. David Jones	1	do	Farmer Own Lands of good Estate
1664	Do Jⁿˢ Dulmage	1	do	do do
1665	Qʳ Master Jⁿˢ Ferguson	1	Ireland	Army
1666	George Smith	1	N. York	Surgeon
1667	Solomon Jones	1	do	Mate[93]
1668	Serjt. Major Martin Kelly	1	do	Labourer
1669	Serjt. Benonee* Wiltse*	1	do	Farmer Leased Land
1670	do Jⁿˢ Simmons	1	do	do do
1671	Corpl. Jⁿˢ Williams	1	do	Labourer
1672	do Jⁿˢ Brooks	1	do	Farmer Own Lands
1673	do Abraham Conklin	1	do	Lease Lands*
1674	Ephraim Jones	1	Massichucets*	Farmer Own Lands
1675	William Snyder	1	N. York	(blank)
	End fo. 163ᵛ (p. 237)			
	Carried Over	75		Christian

NOTES: 91.   While the Ditto was under "lease Lands" it obviously referred to "Farmer".
          92.   Same spelling of "Jeseep" as for No. 1601.
          93.   Likely refers to a "Surgeons Mate".
          No. 1641   See Canadian Genealogist 5:30 (March 1983).

NUMBER	NAMES	INCORPORATED MEN	FROM WHAT PROVINCE OR COUNTRY	REMARKS
	Brought Forward	75		
1676	Christian Abrams	1	New York	Taylor
1677	Andrew Miller	1	do	Labourer
1678	Henry Clark	1	do	do
1679	Abram Rifenbarrick*	1	do	Farmer Lease* Lands
1680	John Alkenbrack	1	do	Labourer
1681	Mathew Thompson	1	do	(blank)
1682	Joseph Griffin	1	do	Taylor Own Lands
1683	James Chambers	1	do	do
1684	Daniel Carr	1	do	Weaver
1685	Fremman Beveley*	1	do	Labourer
1686	Zachary Snider	1	do	do
1687	Jns See	1	do	do
1688	Jns Tuttle	1	do	do
1689	Richard Harris	1	do	Butcher Leased Lands
1690	Jns Lindsey	1	do	Farmer Leased do
1691	Henry Skinkle	1	do	do
1692	James Davis	1	do	Taylor
1693	Adam Earhart*	1	do	Labourer
1694	Amrist* Ferrill	1	do	do
1695	Israel Thompkins	1	do	Farmer Leased Lands
1696	Peter Carpenter	1	do	Labourer
1697	Archibald Nicholason*	1	do	do
1698	James See	1	do	Farmer Leased Lands
1699	Abraham Browne	1	do	do do
1700	Lewis Hix	1	do	do do
1701	Jns Still	1	do	(blank)
1702	Mathias Rose	1	do	Farmer Leased Lands
1703	Jacob Bonisteel	1	do	Labourer
1704	William Rodgers	1	do	Farmer Leased Lands
1705	Jns Scout [94]	1	do	do
1706	Dinnis* Smyth	1	do	Labourer
1707	Jns Simmons	1	do	do
1708	Jns Brisbin	1	do	do
1709	Thimothy* Sales	1	do	Taylor
1710	Baltis Simmons	1	do	Labourer
1711	Marks Snyder	1	do	Farmer Leased Lands
1712	Elie Loneless [95]	1	do	Labourer
1713	Thomas Freeman	1	do	Farmer Own Lands
1714	William Tuttle	1	do	Labourer
1715	Stephen Tuttle	1	do	do
1716	Harmonus See	1	do	do
	End fo. 164 (p. 238)			
	Carried Over	116		Henry

NOTES: 94. 2nd choice Scont.
95. From 1712 to 1716 the names are crowded on the bottom of the page.
Nos. 1998 & 1716 By coincidence, while transcribing these lists, an article in the then current issue of the Record (NYG&B) Vol. 114, Nos. 2 & 3 - & likely No. 4 - has an article on "The See Family". At page 163 are listed, HARMANUS, b. 5 July 1746; JACOBUS, b. 24 Aug 1748; and ABRAHAM, b.c. 1754, as all Loyalists. Also listed is DAVID, bap. 19 Aug 1754. Some spelling varients are SEA/ZEH/CIE. The article suggests the name is Huguenot in origin. Refer to Nos. 664, 1687 and 2200.

NUMBER	NAMES	INCORPORATED MEN	FROM WHAT PROVINCE OR COUNTRY	REMARKS
	Brought Forward	116		
1717	Henry Cole	1	New York	Labourer
1718	Daniel Rose	1	do	do
1719	J^{ns} Earhart	1	do	do
1720	Henry Anderson	1	do	do
1721	Isaac Snyder	1	do	do
1722	Magunw^{s}* Shrader[96]	1	do	do
1723	George Daniel	1	do	do
1724	Serjt. Calep Clanson*	1	do	Labourer
1725	do Conrad Peterson	1	do	do
1726	do Ephraim Ketchem*	1	do	Farmer Leased Land
1727	Nathaniel Corbin	1	Vermount*	do Own Land
1728	Moses Ekins	1	New York	Labourer
1729	J^{ns} A^{rm}* Beard[97]	1	Massichuchets*	Shoemaker
1730	Henry Hewitt	1	do	do
1731	Barnibus Hewit* (see 1730)	1	do	do
1732	Christopher Lake	1	New York	Farmer Own Land
1733	Joseph Stafford	1	Vermount*	Labourer
1734	Esia Hough	1	do	do
1735	Elisha Kinshart	1	do	do
1736	John Garlough	1	do	do
1737	Joseph Rane [98]	1	do	do
1738	Godfrey Charl	1	do	do
1739	Thimothy* Richardson	1	do	do
1740	John Lindey*	1	New York	farmer*
1741	J^{ns} Peter Buntlemass*	1	Conecticut*	Schoolmaster
1742	Josiah Rothburn	1	Vermount*	Labourer
1743	Daniel B. Ayiris*	1	Conecticut*	Schoolmaster
1744	Philip Dulmage	1	New York	(blank)
1745	J^{ns} Sharp	1	do	(blank)
1746	Able Ward	1	do	(blank)
1747	Moses Simons	1	do	(blank)
1748	Daniel Wall	1	Vermount*	Farmer Own Land
1749	Benonie* Wiltse	1	New York	(blank)
1750	William Robins	1	do	(blank)
1751	William Wright	1	do	(blank)
1752	Lieut. Col. J^{ns} Peter as Captn	1	do	Justice of the Peace Own Lands
1753	Lieut. Henry Simons	1	do	Farmer Own Lands
1754	Ensign J^{ns} Peters[99]	1	do	Son to Col^{s} Peters
1755	Serjt. J^{ns} Beach	1	Vermount*	Farmer Own Lands
	End fo. 164v (p. 239)			
	Carried Over	155		Serjeant

NOTES: 96. The writing is quite clear as interpreted.
96. 97. The "A" of "A^{rm}" is quite comparable to the "A" of No. 1720; it is not the "H" of No. 1717, 1730 or 1731.
96. 98. Poor 2nd choice KANE.
96. 99. In No. 1754 the surname in both places is spelled "PETERS"; in No. 1751 "PETER". See Nos. 1795 & 1796.

NUMBER	NAMES	INCORPORATED MEN	FROM WHAT PROVINCE OR COUNTRY	REMARKS
	Brought Forward	155		
1756	Serjeant Franee* Scott	1	New York	Labourer
1757	do William England	1	do	Sawyer
1758	Corpl. Robert Perry	1	Vermount*	Farmer Own Lands
1759	George Chasters	1	N. York	do Lease Lands .
1760	James Froom	1	Vermount*	do Own Lands of good Estate
1761	Jeremiah Mallery	1	do	no Property
1762	Jesse Brown	1	N. York	Farmer Own Lands
1763	Samuel Brownson	1	do	do do
1764	William Belster	1	do	Schollmaster*
1765	Samuel Buck	1	Vermount*	Blacksmith
1766	Abraham Barber	1	New York	Farmer Own Lands
1767	Herkilus Conkrite	1	do	Labourer
1768	Hugh Cameron	1	do	do
1769	William Clark	1	do	Sailor
1770	James Carcallion*	1	do	Labourer
1771	Richard Chambelin*	1	do	Blacksmith
1772	Tice Coons	1	do	Farmer
1773	Edward Elminstone	1	do	Labourer
1774	Kenith Fracer	1	do	do
1775	J<u>ns</u> Falkner	1	do	do
1776	Thomas Goosbury	1	do	do
1777	James Gavin	1	do	do
1778	Jacob Gordiner	1	do	Farmer Own Lands
1779	Jacob Huffnagle	1	do	do Lease Lands
1780	Barnabas Hough	1	Vermount*	Blacksmith
1781	Henry Stóglelon[101]	1	N. York	Labourer
1782	Danid* Harkiman	1	do	Farmer & Shoe Maker
1783	Eligha Hard	1	Vermount*	do Own Lands
1784	Abraham Hillegar	1	New York	Labourer
1785	Abraham Hyatt	1	do	Farmer & Shoe Maker Own Land
1786	Jaimes* Taison	1	do	Schoolmaster
1787	James Kelsey	1	do	Farmer Own Lands of good Estate
1788	J<u>ns</u> Lane	1	do	do
1789	Henry Minard	1	do	Lease Land – of good Estate
1790	Alex<u>r</u> McKenzie	1	do	Labourer
1791	J<u>ns</u> McAuther*	1	do	Farmer & Shoe Maker
1792	J<u>ns</u> McDougle*	1	do	Labourer
1793	J<u>ns</u> McKenny	1	do	Farmer Own Land
	End fo. 165 (p. 240)			
	Carried Over	193		Daniel

NOTES: 101.   2nd choice Stoghelon.   The 2nd "l" is an "l" not a "t".   Considered Stapleton but rejected it.

NUMBER	NAMES	INCORPORATED MEN	FROM WHAT PROVINCE OR COUNTRY	REMARKS
	Brought Forward	193		
1794	Daniel McGillebray*	1	New York	Labourer
1795	Andrew Peters	1	do	Son of Colˢ Peters
1796	Samuel Peters	1	do	do
1797	Christopher Quinn	1	do	Weaver & Farmer
1798	Jⁿˢ Roke*	1	do	Labourer
1799	Mathew Rose	1	do	Farmer Lease Lands
1800	Joseph Robertson	1	do	Weaver
1801	David Scott	1	do	Farmer Own Lands
1802	William Soles	1	do	do Own Lands
1803	Simon Sherman	1	do	Carpenter Lease Land
1804	Robert Smith	1	do	do
1805	Joseph Selee	1	do	Farmer
1806	James Stone	1	do	Labourer
1807	Adam Vint[102]	1	do	Taylor Own House
1808	Jⁿˢ Wainswright	1	do	Labourer
1809	Jⁿˢ Williams	1	do	Farmer Leased Land
1810	Daniel Walker	1	Vermount*	Farmer Own Land of good Estate
1811	Fredrick Warring	1	New York	do Lease Land
1812	Capt. Justus Sherwood	1	Vermount*	Farmer Own Lands
1813	Lieut. James Parrott	1	N. York	do Own Lands
1814	Ensign Elijah Bottom	1	Vermount*	
1815	Serjt. Jⁿˢ Ward	1	do	Farmer Own Lands
1816	do Jⁿˢ Helligar	1	N. York	do Lease Land
1817	Caleb Henderson	1	Vermount*	Farmer Own Lands
1818	Oliver Sweet	1	do	Labourer
1819	John Jacson*	1	N. York	do
1820	Philip Sinitgar*	1	do	do
1821	Andrew Huffnale	1	do	do
1822	William Amsbury	1	Masschehets*	Labourer[103]
1823	Jⁿˢ Bradford	1	do	Labourer
1824	Solomon Ball	1	Vermount*	Farmer & Taylor Own Lands
1825	Nathaniel Brown	1	N. York	Labourer
1826	Shadrai* Ball	1	Vermount*	Farmer
1827	John Brownson	1	do	Taylor
1828	Jacob Ball	1	do	Labourer
1829	Thomas Brown	1	N. York	do
1830	Peter Boyce	1	do	do
1831	Jesse Brown	1	do	Farmer
1832	Charlus Bennit*	1	Vermount*	Blacksmith
	End fo. 165ᵛ (p. 241)			
	Carried Over	232		Silas

NOTES: 102.   2nd choice Dint - poor choice.
            103.   Massachusetts actually written Massehc⸢ᵘᶜ⸣hets.

NUMBER	NAMES	INCORPORATED MEN	FROM WHAT PROVINCE OR COUNTRY	REMARKS
	Brought Forward	232		
1833	Silas Brister	1	New York	Farmer Leased Lands
1834	Adam Cole	1	do	Labourer
1835	Uriah Curtiss	1	Vermount*	Blacksmith Own Lands
1836	John Chester	1	New York	Labourer
1837	Eliphmell Caswell[104]	1	do	do
1838	Levi Danton	1	Machichusetts*	do
1839	William Ferris	1	Boston	do
1840	Adonigah Gillot[105]	1	N. York	Farmer Own Lands
1841	Philip G. Veles[106]	1	do	do & Blacksmith Own Land
1842	Henry Groat	1	do	do Leased Lands
1843	John Halmore	1	do	Labourer
1844	Bruen* Hough	1	do	Labourer
1845	Andrew G. Velei[106]	1	do	Blacksmith
1846	James Hard	1	Vermount*	Labourer
1847	Jⁿˢ Jacobs	1	N. York	do
1848	Canstant* King	1	do	do
1849	Jⁿˢ Knanes	1	do	do
1850	Joseph Louson	1	do	do
1851	Jⁿˢ Linsey	1	do	do
1852	Eugene McSheehy	1	Ireland	do
1853	Cornelius Miller	1	Vermount*	do
1854	Elisha Mallery	1	do	do
1855	Cornelius Mills	1	N. York	do
1856	Lewis Mosher	1	do	Farmer & Shoe Maker
1857	Cornelius Okief* (O'Keefe?)	1	do	Labourer
1858	Jⁿˢ Okes	1	Vermount*	do
1859	William Parker	1	N. York	do
1860	Henry Radeker*	1	do	do
1861	William Sleter[107]	1	Ireland	do
1862	Samuel Sherwood	1	N. York	Farmer Lease Lands
1863	Justis* Selee*	1	Conecticut*	Labourer
1864	Asahell Trumble	1	Vermount*	do
1865	Thomas Wood	1	do	Farmer
1866	Thomas Welsh	1	N. York	Labourer
1867	Joseph White	1	Vermount*	Farmer Own Lands
1868	Jonathⁿ Wickwire	1	N. York	a House & Own Land
1869	Jacob Waidrad*	1	do	Labourer
1870	Michael Whallen	1	do	do
	End fo. 166 (p. 242)			
	Carried Over	270		Joseph

NOTES: 104. 2nd choice Eliphinell.
105. 2nd choice Adonifah.
106. Defintely VELE + one other possible letter - an "s", or an "i" or even an "d".
107. A small ink blot is at the bottom of the 2nd letter in the surname; thus, 2nd choice SHETER - the other letters not in doubt. SLATER ?
No. 1845 most likely VELEI; 2nd choice VELEL.
No. 1869 - 2nd choice WALDRAD.

NUMBER	NAMES	INCORPORATED MEN	FROM WHAT PROVINCE OR COUNTRY	REMARKS
	Brought Forward	270		
1871	Joseph White Jun.ʳ	1	Vermount*	Farmer
1872	Russel Pitman	1	do	Labourer
1873	Capt.ⁿ Jonathon Jones	1	N. York	Justice of the Peace Own Lands
1874	Lieut. Gosham French[108]	1	do	Merchant & Own Land
1875	Ensign Thomas Sherwood	1	do	Farmer Own Lands
1876	Serjt. Elikie* Northrip	1	do	do Own Land
1877	do Peter Carrigan	1	do	Weaver
1878	do David Williams	1	(blank)	Blacksmith
1879	Corpl. Henry Tinkel*	1	N. York	Farmer
1880	James Wiltsie	1	do	Labourer
1881	Conrad Rosman	1	do	Farmer Own Lands
1882	Thomas Crisdell	1	do	(blank)
1883	Jacob Thompson	1	do	Farmer
1884	Enoch Mallery	1	Vermount*	do Own Lands
1885	Elkanan* Rabbet*	1	Massichuchets*	Blacksmith
1886	Christopher Mosier	1	N. York	Farmer Lease Land
1887	Jerid Tylor	1	Massichuchets	Carpenter Own Lands
1888	Simon Snyder	1	New York	Farmer Lease Land
1889	Thomas Jones	1	do	(blank)
1890	David Logan	1	do	Farmer Own Lands
1891	Jonathas Phelps	1	do	do Lease Land
1892	Fredᵏ Baker	1	do	do
1893	David Huffman	1	do	do
1894	Joseph Goodmelly*	1	do	Blacksmith
1895	Trulove Buttler*	1	do	do & Farmer Own Land
1896	Jⁿˢ Allen	1	do	Butcher
1897	Daniel Beagle	1	do	Carpenter
1898	Jⁿˢ Pork*	1	do	Labourer
1899	Martin Stover	1	do	Farmer Lease Land
1900	Philip Bonesteell*	1	do	Do Do
1901	Paul Carrigan	1	do	Weaver
1902	George Pool	1	do	Farmer
1903	Abraham Crawsin*	1	do	do Lease Land
1904	Daniel Eollon*	1	do	Labourer
1905	Samuel Dunham	1	do	Farmer
1906	Peter Eselstine*	1	do	do Lease Land
	End fo. 166ᵛ (p. 243)			
	Carried Over	306		Jⁿᵒ

NOTES: 108. 2nd choice Gasham.
Nos. 1703 & 1900   See NYG&B Record Vol. 114, No. 3, pages 167 & 170; Round Top Lutheran Baptisms (Town of Pine Plains, Dutchess Co., New York) as to a clue of possible origins of this name in America. The spelling is Johanes BOHNESTIEL and Elisabeth BONESTIEL.

NUMBER	NAMES	INCORPORATED MEN	FROM WHAT PROVINCE OR COUNTRY	REMARKS
	Brought Forward	306		
1907	J^{ns} Colbreth	1	N. York	Farmer
1908	J^{ns} McKinzie*	1	do	do Lease Lands
1909	Archibald McNeal	1	do	do
1910	Joseph Enery[109]	1	do	Labourer
1911	James Bivins	1	do	do
1912	William White	1	do	Farmer Leased Lands
1913	Syx* Hatchellor	1	do	do do
1914	Aron* Bull	1	Vermount*	do Own Land
1915	Darby Sillick	1	do	do
1916	Joseph Tuttle	1	do	Labourer
1917	Thomas Fracer Junr	1	do	do
1918	William Williston	1	Vermount*	Farmer
1919	George Hutchonson	1	New York	Labourer
1920	J^{ns} Whitley	1	N. York	Farmer
1921	Joseph Kingsbury	1	do	do Lease Lands
1922	James Colliard	1	do	Carpenter
1923	J^{ns} Sharp	1	do	Farmer
1924	Amos Holstead[110]	1	do	do
1925	Abram Bolton	1	do	do
1926	Nathan^l Tuttle	1	do	do
1927	Jacob Cowdey	1	do	do
1928	Peter Freeman	1	do	Farmer
1929	J^{ns} Havens	1	do	do Lease Land
1930	William Fraser 2^D [111]	1	do	(blank)
1931	Benjimin Betts	1	do	Carpenter
1932	Benjamin* Eastman	1	Vermount*	Labourer
1933	Norris Bisco	1	do	do
1934	James Johnson	1	N. York	Farmer
1935	William Williston	1	Vermount*	do Own Estate
1936	Thomas Fraser	1	N. York	(blank)
1937	Alexer* McEntosh*	1	do	Farmer
1938	William Fraser 3^D [111]	1	do	Taylor
1939	Richd Turner	1	do	Labourer
1940	J^{ns} Woodburn	1	Rode* Island	do
1941	William Fraser 1st [111]	1	New York	(blank)
1942	Azur* Northrip	1	do	Labourer
1943	Joseph Hosier	1	do	do
1944	Thomas Oar[112]	1	do	Taylor
1945	Allin* Campbell	1	do	Schoolmaster
1946	Phils Hard[113]	1	Vermount*	Farmer Own Lands
1947	Daniel Simmons	1	N. York	(blank)
	End fo. 167 (p. 244)			
	Carried Over	437		Robert

NOTES: 109.   2nd choice EVERY.
110.   2nd choice HOLSTEED.
111.   One might assume that this is the second and third man of this name in the list. The first man of this name is at No. 1941.
112.   2nd choice DAR - poor choice.
113.   PHILIP ?

NUMBER	NAMES	INCORPORATED MEN	FROM WHAT PROVINCE OR COUNTRY	REMARKS
	Brought Forward	347		
1948	Robert Clarke	1	N. York	Milwright Own Lands
1949	Archibald Nichol(a)son[114]	1	do	Labourer
1950	Jacob Hess	1	do	do
1951	Moses Hunter	1	do	do
1952	Richd Hanly	1	Vermount*	Farmer & Carpenter
1953	David Scott	1	N. York	do
1954	Ebeze* King	1	do	do Own Lands
1955	J^ns Leep	1	do	do
1956	J^ns McDougall	1	do	do Own Lands
1957	John Millus[115]	1	do	Labourer
1958	J^ns Scout	1	do	Farmer
1959	J^ns Shorty	1	do	do
1960	Daniel Scott	1	Vermount*	do Own Lands
1961	Robt. Whetman	1	N. York	do Lease Lands
1962	John Hand	1	do	Labourer
1963	Nicholas Huffman	1	do	Farmer
1964	Benjimin Light	1	do	Blacksmith
1965	Jonas Amey	1	do	Farmer Leased Lands
1966	Andrew Brown	1	do	Carpenter Leased Lands
1967	Thomas Comer	1	do	Farmer Lease Lands
1968	Silas Hamlin	1	do	do
1969	James Brunson	1	do	Labourer
1970	Neal* Scott	1	do	do
1971	William Jones	1	do	(blank)
1972	Jobest Huffman[116]	1	do	Farmer
1973	Nicholas Amey	1	do	do Lease Lands
1974	Capt. William Fracor*	1	do	Farmer Owne* Lands
1975	Lieut. Gideon Adams	1	do	do Own Lands
1976	do Edward Jeseep[92]	1	do	(blank)
1977	Serjt. Ebenezer Washburn*	1	Vermount*	Farmer Own Lands
1978	do J^ns Smyth	1	New York	do Lease Lands
1979	do Ephraim Curry	1	do	do do
1980	Corpl. Abraham Ostrander	1	do	(blank)
1981	David Hunter	1	do	do Lease Lands
1982	Wm Clow	1	do	do do
1983	James McHmoyl[117]	1	do	do & Carpenter
1984	William Fracer	1	do	Labourer
1985	Thomas Fracer	1	do	do
1986	Benjamin Davis	1	do	Farmer
1987	Elisha Russell	1	do	do
	End fo. 167^v (p. 245)			
	Carried Over	387		Dunham

NOTES: 114. The "a" is inserted with an inverted "v".
        115. 2nd choice MILLIAS.
        116. 2nd choice JOHEST.
        117. The problem with this name is that the "H" is overwritten; the other letters are quite distinct. See No. 2013.

NUMBER	NAMES	INCORPORATED MEN	FROM WHAT PROVINCE OR COUNTRY	REMARKS
	Brought Forward	387		
1988	Dunham Pettit	1	N. York	Blacksmith
1989	J^{ns} Eselstine	1	do	Farmer Lease Lands
1990	Gilbert Storm	1	do	do do
1991	Edmond Frost	1	do	do do
1992	Peter Hugdone	1	do	Labourer
1993	J^{ns} Snyder	1	do	do
1994	J^{ns} Huntly	1	do	do
1995	J^{ns} Green	1	do	Farmer Lease Land
1996	J^{ns} Van Camp	1	do	Labourer
1997	Valentine Herman	1	do	Farmer
1998	J^{ns} Gillist	1	do	do
1999	Christopher Germain	1	do	Labourer
2000	J^{ns} Germain Junr	1	do	do
2001	Jonathan Harris	1	do	do
2002	J^{ns} Dixon	1	do	Farmer Lease Land
2003	Ezekial Spicer Junr	1	do	Labourer
2004	Daniel Carr	1	do	(blank)
2005	Thomas Jones	1	do	(blank)
2006	Joshua Loussey*	1	do	Farmer Own Land
2007	Milo Webster	1	do	Labourer
2008	Banjamin Drake	1	do	do
2009	J^{ns} Dawsen	1	do	do
2010	Capt. Peter Drummond	1	do	(blank)
2011	Ensign Thomas Man	1	do	(blank)
2012	Serjt. Duncan Robertson	1	do	Labourer
2013	do Hugh McHnoyle[117]	1	do	Carpenter
2014	do Jeremiah Frances	1	England	Blacksmith
2015	Corpl. Henry French	1	Vermount*	Farmer Own Land
2016	do Gilbert Hayot	1	N. York	Shoe Maker
2017	do J^{ns} Fitzgerald	1	Ireland	Clark*
2018	Collin McKenzie	1	N. York	Labourer
2019	J^{ns} Gray	1	do	do
2020	William Smith	1	Boston	Merchant
2021	J^{ns} Hogle	1	New York	(blank)
2022	George Hogle	1	do	(blank)
	End fo. 168 (p. 246)			
	Carried Over	422		Capt.

NOTES: 117. No. 2013 is no clearer than No. 1983.

NUMBER	NAMES	INCORPORATED MEN	FROM WHAT PROVINCE OR COUNTRY	REMARKS
	Brought Forward	422		
2023	Capt. Jⁿˢ Jones	1	New York	Farmer Own Lands of good Estate
2024	Lieut. Alexʳ Campbell	1	do	do do do do
2025	Ensign Jⁿˢ Dusinberg	1	do	do
2026	Serjt. Jⁿᵒ Cilchrist*	1	do	do Own Lands
2027	do Daniel Dunham	1	do	do do
2028	do Thomas McKnight	1	do	do
2029	Corpˡ Jⁿˢ Germain	1	do	do
2030	do Alexʳ McNail*	1	do	do Leased Lands
2031	do Jⁿˢ Shibley	1	do	do do
2032	Lozie Blancher	1	do	(blank)
2033	Abraham Snyder	1	do	Labourer
2034	Thomas Jackson	1	do	do
2035	David Harney	1	do	Shoe Maker
2036	William Sanders	1	do	Labourer
2037	Chatwell Persons	1	Conecticut*	Farmer Own Lands
2038	Solomon Dunham	1	N. York	Labourer
2039	Duncan Grant	1	Vermount*	(blank)
2040	Daniel McAchron*	1	N. York	Farmer Own Land
2041	Peter Snyder	1	do	Labourer
2042	William Leahy	1	do	do
2043	Simon V. Camp	1	do	Farmer Leased Lands
2044	Simon Stone	1	do	Labourer
2045	James Robertson	1	Boston	do
2046	Aron Watson	1	do	Wheelwrite Own Land
2047	Alexʳ Hays¹¹⁸	1	Vermount*	Labourer
2048	Daniel Spicer	1	N. York	do
2049	Ezekial Spicer Senʳ	1	do	Farmer Leased Land
2050	Jacob Van Camp	1	do	do do
2051	Jamis* Van Camp	1	do	do Labourer*
2052	John Michael	1	do	Farmer
2053	Abraham Tinkey	1	do	Labourer
2054	William Copeland	1	do	Carpenter
2055	Peter Daly	1	do	Labourer
2056	James Jackson	1	do	Farmer Leased Lands
2057	Tunis Heagerman	1	do	Labourer
	End fo. 168ᵛ (p. 247)			
	Carried Over	457		Peter

NOTES: 118. 2nd choice HOYS.
          No. 2040 - misspelling ? for McEACHEN.
          No. 2026 - GILCHRIST ?
          No. 2043 - VAN CAMP ?

NUMBER	NAMES	INCORPORATED MEN	FROM WHAT PROVINCE OR COUNTRY	REMARKS
	Brought Forward	457		
2058	Peter Thomas	1	N. York	Farmer
2059	Stephen Boyce	1	do	Labourer
2060	J^{ns} Conklin	1	do	do
2061	David Beaty	1	do	Farmer
2062	Gilbert Jeimie	1	do	Labourer
2063	Jesper More	1	do	Farmer
2064	Samuel White	1	Berbadoes*	Labourer
2065	Simon Hard	1	Vermount*	do
2066	Capt. J^{ns} Wm Meyers	1	N. York	Farmer Own Land
2067	Lieut. J^{ns} Riter	1	do	do do
2068	Ensign Harmonus Pest	1	do	do
2069	Serjeant Robert Simpson	1	do	Blacksmith
2070	do George Rouse	1	do	Farmer Lease Lands
2071	do Joseph Knap	1	do	do
2072	Corpl. Jahomas* Burris	1	do	do
2073	do Jacob Thomas	1	do	Labourer
2074	Nicholas Mosier	1	do	Farmer
2075	David Mitchell	1	do	(blank)
2076	Isaac Houghtail	1	do	Farmer
2077	James Mead	1	do	Labourer
2078	Church Brown	1	Conecticut*	do
2079	Joshua Brownell	1	N. York	do
2080	J^{ns} Mock	1	do	Farmer
2081	Christopher Houghtail	1	do	Labourer
2082	Thomas Lestor	1	do	Farmer
2083	Everhart Wagner	1	do	do
2084	J^{ns} Lighthart	1	do	Labourer
2085	J^{ns} Colwell	1	do	do
2086	J^{no} Boge	1	do	do
2087	Cornelius Hoyatt	1	do	do
2088	Edward Hogans	1	do	(blank)
2089	Samuel Holunbrooke[119]	1	do	Farmer
2090	George Richman	1	do	Taylor
2091	Alex^{r} Bernet*	1	do	Labourer
2092	J^{ns} Gervey	1	do	do
2093	Isac* Valentine	1	do	do
2094	Cornelius Lossie	1	do	(blank)
2095	Thimothy Porter	1	Vermount*	Labourer
2096	Rosewell Gay	1	New York	do
2097	Jacob Kosinbrook	1	do	do
2098	Philip Smith	1	do	do
2099	William Witherwax	1	do	Farmer
	End fo. 169 (p. 248)			
	Carried Over	499		Frances

NOTES: 119. There is an ink smudge here - could be HOLLINBROOKE.

NUMBER	NAMES	INCORPORATED MEN	FROM WHAT PROVINCE OR COUNTRY	REMARKS
	Brought Forward	499		
2100	Frances Hogle	1	New York	(blank)
2101	Henry Jackson	1	do	Farmer
2102	J^ns Ferguson	1	do	(blank)
2103	Ephraim Proctor	1	Boston	Farmer Own Land
2104	Nicholas Loucks	1	N. York	Labourer
2105	Samuel Wearthead*	1	Barbadoes	do
2106	Robert Gordiner	1	N. York	do
2107	Samuel Beekman	1	do	do
2108	Peter Gilchrist*	1	do	Farmer & Shoemaker
2109	Nathaniel Osburn[120]	1	Vermount*	Labourer
2110	J^ns McMaaugh*	1	Irland*	do
2111	J^ns Smith	1	N. York	do
2112	J^ns Davis	1	do	do
2113	Ephraim Eyers	1	Vermount*	Farmer
2114	Antony Earnest	1	N. York	Labourer
2115	J^ns Cleaneland	1	do	do
2116	Bartholomew Carly	1	do	Farmer
2117	Cyril Ried	1	do	Blacksmith
2118	Hose More	1	do	Carpenter
2119	Michael Conner	1	do	Farmer
2120	James Gray	1	do	do
2121	Abijah Hawley	1	Vermount*	do Own Land
2122	J^ns Everhart	1	New York	Labourer
2123	Rowland Lennox	1	do	do
2124	Duncan Cameron	1	do	do
2125	J^ns Ruddenback	1	do	do* Lease Land
2126	J^ns Bottwood	1	Vermount*	Labourer
2127	David Dulmage	1	N. York	Carpenter & Farmer
2128	J^ns McPherson	1	do	Farmer
2129	William Perry	1	do	do Leased Land
2130	Jadock Hauly[121]	1	Vermount*	Labourer
2131	David Falhammer	1	N. York	do
2132	Gabriel Valentine	1	do	do
2133	Aaron Sampson	1	Vermount*	Farmer Own Land
2134	Theop^h Sampson	1	do	Labourer
2135	George Weymire	1	New York	do
2136	J^ns Brown	1	do	Farmer
	End fo. 169^v (p. 249)			
	Carried Over	536		Daniel

NOTES: 120. Likely meant to be OSBORN - but definitely OSB- -N.
         121. Compare with No. 2121.

         No. 2131 - COLHAMMER ?

NUMBER	NAMES	INCORPORATED MEN	FROM WHAT PROVINCE OR COUNTRY	REMARKS
	Brought Forward	536		
2137	Daniel York	1	New York	Labourer
2138	Oliver Bratt	1	do	Carpenter
2139	Calep Nelson	1	do	Labourer
2140	Robert Trip	1	do	Cooper
2141	James Jerolemy*	1	do	(blank)
2142	William Bustead	1	do	Farmer
2143	J<u>ns</u> Bleakly	1	do	Blacksmith
2144	Abram Lampman[31]	1	do	Labourer
2145	Jobes* Bernheart	1	do	do
2146	J<u>ns</u> Sulfrage	1	do	do
2147	David Michael	1	do	do
2148	Henry Shuffet	1	do	do
2149	James Worrick	1	do	(blank)
2150	J<u>ns</u> Valentine	1	do	(blank)
2151	Phils Norton	1	Vermount*	(blank)
2152	W<u>m</u> Hen. Shoughnessey[122]	1	N. York	Farmer
2153	Peter Plass	1	do	Shoemaker
2154	Thomas Barton	1	do	Farmer Own Lands
2155	Abraham Coons	1	do	Labourer
2156	Abraham Sanders	1	do	do
2157	Rubin Sherwood	1	do	(blank)
2158	Capt. Thomas Fraser.	1	N. York	Farmer Own Lands of good Estate
2159	Lieut. James Robins	1	do	do & Trader Leased Lands do
2160	Ensign William Lampson	1	do	(blank)
2161	Serjt. Duncan McAlpin	1	do	Labourer
2162	do Charlus Ross	1	do	Farmer
2163	do Duncan McGregor	1	do	do
2164	Corpl. Philip Sharp	1	do	do
2165	do David Craford*	1	Vermount*	do
2166	Jacob German	1	New York	(blank)
2167	William Fraser	1	do	(blank)
2168	James Humphry	1	do	Farmer
2169	Armstrong Williams	1	do	do
2170	Abraham Scott	1	do	do
	End fo. 170 (p. 250)			
	Carried Over	570		George

NOTES: 122. William Henry presumed.

NUMBER	NAMES	INCORPORATED MEN	FROM WHAT PROVINCE OR COUNTRY	REMARKS
	Brought Forward	570		
2171	George Stars	1	Massichuchets*	Farmer
2172	Peter McPherson	1	New York	do Leased Lands
2173	Henry Mott	1	do	do
2174	John McMullen	1	do	Labourer
2175	Conrad Fridret	1	do	Farmer
2176	Everit Ostrander	1	do	' Labourer
2177	John Andrews	1	do	do
2178	Jacob Andrews	1	do	do
2179	John Partlow	1	do	do
2180	Jⁿˢ Percy	1	do	do
2181	Jⁿˢ Crysdal	1	do	Farmer Leased Land
2182	James Fracer	1	do	Labourer
2183	Jⁿˢ West	1	do	Farmer Lease Land
2184	William Toehout	1	do	do Lease Land
2185	James Adams	1	do	Labourer
2186	Henry Clumb	1	do	Farmer Own Lands
2187	Adam Vanderhider	1	do	Labourer
2188	Jacob Carpenter	1	do	do
2189	William Saunders	1	do	Farmer
2190	Henry Sanders Junr[123]	1	do	Labourer
2191	Jⁿˢ Woghuff*	1	do	Miller
2192	Peter Suurr[124]	1	do	Labourers*
2193	Jeremiah Fraser	1	do	do
2194	Thomas Sherer	1	do	Farmer
2195	Frances Ball	1	do	Labourer
2196	William Maxwell	1	do	do
2197	Alexʳ McDonold	1	do	(blank)
2198	Hugh Cameron	1	do	Labourer
2199	Cary Pitman	1	do	do
2200	David See[125]	1	Vermount*	Farmer
2201	Daniel Davis	1	do	Labourer
2202	William Sanders	1	N. York	(blank)
2203	Rubin Mott	1	do	Farmer
	End fo. 170ᵛ (p. 251)			
	Total of Loyal Rangers	603		Original*

NOTES: 123. Compare with No. 2189; suggests SAUNDERS & SANDERS are same name when they follow one another.
124. Poor 2nd choice SHURR.
125. See Nos. 664, 1687, 1698 & 1716. The NYG&B article gave an alternate name for JACOBUS as JAMES - but they were all from New York. This, DAVID, is from Vermont - or is this an error ?

End of Volume* (Printed in handwriting - not part of the original writing)

INDEX

AARSH, Joseph	898	ANSLEY, Amos	148
ABLE, Henry	1009	ANTHONY	
		John	992
ABRAHAMS/ABRAMS		Richard	903
Andrew	117		
Christian	1676	APPLEBEE, William	355
ADAMS		ARMSTRONG	
Andrew	924	Jesse	404
Lieut. Gideon	1975	Jonathon	1164
James	889,2185	William	580
Joel	931		
Mrs. Lt.	584	ASH, Peter	823
Mr.	151		
Samuel	603	ASTEN, Jacob	1453
William	932		
Mrs. William	524	ATKINSON, Lt. William	390
ADONIFAH, Gillot	1840	ATLIK, Samuel	833
AILSWORTH, Joseph	469	AULT	
		Ener/Ever/Euer	1186
AIRS, Ephriem	137	John	1190
		Michael	1392
ALABACK, Lt. Emmanuel	391	Nicholas	1395
ALBRANT		AYIRIS, Daniel B.	1743
Frances	1389		
Hank	1485		
ALGIRE/ALGUIRE, Martin	1118	BABEETY, Mrs.	183
ALKENBRACK, John	1680	BAKER	
		Adam	1107
ALLEN		Conrad	1430
John	1896	Fredrick	1892
Joseph	694	Henry	1242
		John	438
ALLISON, Joseph	426	William	1429
ALLSWORTH, Joseph	469	BALL	
		Frances	2195
AMAN, Jacob	1515	Jacob	1828
		Shadrai	1826
AMEY		Solomon	1824
Jonas	606,1965		
Nicholas	604,1973	BANGELL/BANGLE	
		Adam	1542
AMON, John	1486	Abrahams	745
		John	1442
AMSBURY, William	314,1822	Henry	1554
		William	1553
ANDERSON			
Captain	1345	BARBER, Abraham(s)	745,1766
Ebenezer	1193		
Elisha	1192	BARLOW, Abner	899
Henry	1720		
James	180	BARNET (see BERNET)	
John	259	Mrs.	1
ANDREW/ANDREWS		BARNHURT (try BERNHEART)	
Jacob	2178	Joseph	994
John	598,738,2177		
Thomas	60	BARNUM, Levi	895
ANNA, John	95	BARRET, Stephen	261
ANNABLE, Serjeant John	1350	BARTHS, Cathrine	317

100

BARTON, Thomas	2154		BISHOP, John	1264

BARTON, Thomas 2154

BASTEDO, Jacob 2

BATISE, Widow 186

BAXTER, William 1162

BEACH
John 744
Serjt. John 1755

BEACHER, Solomon 134

BEAGLE, Daniel 775,1897

BEARD, John Arm. 1729

BEARS, Jacob 120

BEATON, Angus 1332

BEATY, David 2061

BECKER, Conrad 1276

BEEBY, Peter 267

BEEKMAN, Samuel 2107

BELL
Duncan 961
William 485

BELSTER, William 1764

BENEDICK,
Elijah 262
John 1244
Serjt. Joseph 1384

BENNIT/BENNITT
Charlus 1832
Ephriam 988,187
William 506

BENSON, Mathew 435

BENTER, Henry 475

BERNET (see BURNET)
Alexander 2091

BERNHEART (see BARNHURT)
Jobes 2145
Mrs. 613

BEST, Conrad 1603

BETS/BETTS
Benjamin 610,1931

BEVERLEY/BEVERLY
David 1245
Freeman 1685

BILL (see 170, 804)
William 808

BISCO, Norris 1933

BISHOP, John 1264

BIVINS, James 1911

BLAKELY, James 368

BLANCHER, Lozie 2032

BLASKSLAY, John 746

BLEAKLY, John 2143

BLISS, John 880

BLUNT, Margt. 3

BOARDER, Mrs. 350

BOEN (BOWEN ? - see 316)
Luke 1113

BOGE, John 2086

BOGERT, Gibert 486

BOICE (see BOYCE)
Andrew 1325
John 1110
Widow 740

BOLTON, Abraham 1925

BONEN (see 1113)
Luckus 316

BONESTEEL/BONISTEEL
Jacob 1703
Philip 1900

BORGHAM, Lurd 883

BOTHERBACK, John 780

BOTHWICK, Joshua 260

BOTTOM, Ensign Elijah 1814

BOTTWOOD 2126

BOUCH/BOUCK
Adam 1533
David 1149
Fredrick 1145,1371
John 1317

BOWKER, John 1262

BOWMAN
Adam 609
Elizabeth 74

BOYCE (see BOICE)
Peter 1830
Stephen 2059

BOYLE, George 269

BRADFORD, John 1823

BYRNS, Gerrit	1147		CARPENTER	
			Jacob	2188
			Peter	1696
CADMAN				
John Junior	1504		CARR	
John Senior	1503		Daniel/Daniels	749,1684,
				2004
CAHE, Henry	1330		Mrs.	6
CALDER			CARRIGAN	
Fredrick	974		Paul	1901
William	977		Serjt. Peter	1877
William	1208		William	940
CALDWELL, Robert	192		CARSCALION/CARSCALLION	
			(see CARCALLION)	
CAMERON/CAMORAN			Edward	1623
(see CARMERON)			Edward Pensioner	370
Alexander	195,319,			
	1315,1539		CARSON, Thomas	10
Daniel	844			
Duncan	369,1626,		CARTWRIGHT	
	2124		Mrs.	9
Even/Evern	1189		Richard	1610
Hugh	167,1768,			
	2198		CASE	
John	11,378,		Corpl. Joseph	1353
	1207,1541		Josiah	1631
John & Nancy	786			
			CASS (see CASSE)	
CAMPBELL/CAMBELL			John	1276
Alexander	14,531		Jonah	616
Lieut. Alexander	2024			
Allin	1945		CASSE, Drummer Elazer	1406
Serjt. Daniel	1197			
Donald	1217		CASTLE	
Duncan	273		Lemuel	196
George	894		Mrs.	535
James	98,747,			
	1625		CASTLEMAN/CASTLMAN	
John	138		Adam	1279
Mary	73		Conrad	1280
Mrs.	7,599		Henry	1343
William	461,1311		Richard	1303
			Sefrenius	1273
CAMP (VAN CAMP ?)			Thomas	1476
Simon V.	2043		Vernor	1408
			William	1282
CANE, Henry	1330			
			CASTWELL, David	1646
CARCALLION (see CARSCALION)				
James	1770		CASWELL	
			Eliphmell	1837
CARHOMHORN, Peter	1484		Samuel	964
CARKNER, John	923		CATCHAPAH/CATCHAPAK	
			Henry	989
CARLY				
Bartholomew	2116		CATCHEM (KETCHEM ?)	
Mrs.	534		David	1440
CARMAN/CARMEN			CAVAN, Thomas	88
John	448			
Michael/Micheal	12,318		CAYSER (KEYSER ?)	
	1112		John	1365
CARMERON (CAMERON ?)			Michael	1366
Mrs.	536			
			CEAREY/CEEREY	
			Richard	1496

CHAMBELIN, Richard	1771
CHAMBERS	
James	748,1683
John	271
CHAPMAN, John	446
CHAPPLE, Hirum	947
Charl, Godfrey	1738
Chasters, George	1759
CHESHER (CHESTER ?)	
John	371
CHESTER, John	1836
CHILCHRIST (see GILCHRIST/	
CILCHRIST)	
Catherine	578
Peter	628
CHILTON, Robert T.	272
CHISLOM (CHISHOLM ?)	
Alexander	1526
William	320,1531
CHRISDELL (see 537)	
Thomas	1882
CILCHRIST (GILCHRIST ?)	
Serjt. John	2026
CLAIM, 2nd Lt. John	678
CLANSON, Serjt. Calep	1724
CLARK/CLARKE	
Frances	1550
Henry	1678
Serjt. James	1472
Robert	1948
William	489,1769
CLASM, 2nd Lt. John	678
CLAWSON, Caleb	270
CLEANELAND, John	2115
CLEMONS, John	874
CLINE (see KLINE)	
Adam	1314
Philip	1501
CLINTCH, Benjamin	501
CLOW	
Henry	601,742
William	1982
CLUCK, John	467
CLUMB, Henry	2186
CODNER, Johnmal	845

COLBREATH/COLBRETH	
Mrs.	597
John	1907
COLE	
Adam	1834
Daniel	702
Elias	721
Frances	1488
Henry	1717
John	720
John Junior	731
Simon T.	1637
COLHAMMER (see HAMMER,	
try 2131)	
George	1018
COLLARD, Abraham	516
COLLIARD, James	1922
COLLIER, Richard	700
COLWELL, John	2085
COMER, Thomas	321,1967
CONELY	
John	906
William	1322
CONEY, Samuel	193
CONINE, Leonard	681
CONKLIN	
Abraham	362
Corpl. Abraham	1673
John	2060
CONKRITE, Herkilus	1767
CONNER, Michael	2119
CONRAD, Robert	398
COOK	
Jacob	522
Mary Widow	197
Philip	509,1260
Thomas	274
COON/COONS (otherwise KUHN)	
Abraham	2155
Casper	1439
Conrad	1397
Jacob	351,1116
John	1467
Tice	1772
COPELAND, William	2054
CORBIN, Nathaniel	198,1727
CORNWALL,	
Albert	437
Thomas	993
CORRY, James	191

COSBEY, George 904

COSS, Petter 1511

COSTELLO, Cathr. 15

COTTER, James 1219

COTTOM, William 1163

COUCKHILL, Joseph 66

COUGHNOT, John 111

COUGH, John 13

COULTER, Andrew 533

COUNTRYMAN (formerly LANDMAN)
Corpl. Jacob 1473

COURTNEY, Dennis 1248

COVEL, Simon 1660

COVEY, Samuel 193

COWDEY, Jacob 1927

CRABTREE, John 1458

CRAFORD/CRAWFORD
Corpl. David 2165
George 156
John 1378,1507

CRAWSIN, Abraham 1903

CREIGHTON, William 155

CRELLER, Peter 934

CRISTE, Ralph 158

CRITERMAN (see CRYTERMAN)
Corpl. Jacob 1474

CROMP, Thomas 8

CRONDER, James 1532

CROOKSHANKS, Wm. 4

CROSS
Henry 905
John 194,851

CROUDER (see CROWDER)
Isaac 1557
James 1532

CROUSE
John 1274
Peter 1106

CROWDER (try CROUDER)
Mrs. 614
William 615

CRUTHERS, Mrs. 5

CRYSDAL (see next two entries)
John 2181

CRYSLOR (CRYSLER ?)
John 1140

CRYSODEL (CRYSLER ?)
Mrs. 537

CRYTERMAN (see CRITERMAN)
Harmonus 1428
Joseph 1367

CRYTES, George 1421

CULBERT, MRS. 171

CURRY
Serjt. Ephraim 1979
James 939
John 945

CURTISS
Mrs. 532
Uriah 1835

DAFOE (see DAVOE/DEFOE)
Abraham 965,972
Daniel 980
Jacob 971
John 1012
Michael 979

DALY
Peter 2055
William 1176

DAMSEN, James 456

DANIEL, George 1723

DANLEY, Carlus 415

DANNIS, Corpl. Nicholas 1385

DANTON, Levi 1838

DAR, Thomas 1944

DARRAK, James 275

DAVIES, Richard 684

DAVIS
Abel 944
Benjamin 1986
Daniel 2201
Hendrick 1431
James 1692
John 1254,2112
Jothan 927
Peter 1128
Richard 322
Robert 1114

DAVOE (see DAFOE/DEFOE)
Conrad 1437
Martin 928

DAVY, John	1344
DAWN, Joseph	708
DAWSEN, John	2009
DAY, Barnabas	408
DEAN	
Moses	494
Lt. Samuel	493
DEATLOR (see DETLOR)	
John	162
DEDRICK	
Friday	106
Michael	513
DEFOE (see DAFOE/DAVOE)	
John	1635
John Pensioner	200
DEFOREST, Mrs.	16
DELANEY, Stephen Esquire	709
DELYA, Peter	484
DEMERA, David	436
DEMIT, Garret	618
DEMON (try DIMON)	
Jacob Jnr.	907
DERLAND, Philip	701
DERRICK	
Conrad	990
Philip/PHILLIP	199,991
DETLOR (see DEATLOR)	
Petor	278
DIBBLE, Asa	933
DIMON (DIAMOND?)	
Jacob	379,986
John	279
DINGWELL	
James	1468
John	1493
DINNEY, Jacob	1463
DIXON, John	617,2002
DOBBS, Michael	447
DONALLY (try DANLEY)	
Mary	53
DOP	
Adam	1133
Peter	1127
DORN	
David	1168

DORN (continued)	
Jacob	1115
Jeremiah	1167
Mordica	462
DORSEY, (Capt.?) Thomas	457
DOUGHERTY, William	1509
DOUGLAS (see DUGHAS)	
John	277
DRAKE, Benjamin	2008
DRIVER, John	688
DRUMMOND, Capt. Peter	2010
DUER (DEWER?)	
John	1538
DUCOLEN/DUCOLERS, Stephen	372
DUGHAS/DUGHASS/DUGLAS(S)	
John	277
Robert	276
DULMAGE	
David	2127
Lieut. John	1664
Philip	1744
DUNBAR, Susan	150
DUNHAM	
Serjt. Daniel	2027
Daniels	751
Samuel	1905
Solomon	2038
DUNN, Richard	705
DUNON, Jacob	986
DURLING, Thomas	483
DUSINBERG, Ensign John	2025
DUSLER, Andrew	1135
DYER	
Bt.	105
John	423
EARHART	
Adam	1693
John	1719
EARNEST, Anthony	2114
EARTMAY/EEARTMAY	
Benjamin	620
EDGE, Daniel	946
EDY, Daniel	203
EICHLES, William	687

EKINS, Moses	1728
ELLOMS, John	1281
ELMINSTONE, Edward	1773
EMBURY, Mrs.	67
EMERY, Laurence	122

EMPEY/EMPY (otherwise IMPEY)

Adam	1441
Corpl. (John F. ?)	1204
Serjt. John	1383
Philip	1414
Corpl. Philip	1351
Stophel (Christopher)	1422
William	1418

ENERY, Joseph	1910
ENETS, Roswell	280

ENGLAND

William	147,619
Serjt. William	1757♦

EOLLON, Daniel	1904

ESELTINE (see VANALSTINE)

John	1989
Peter	1906

ESLING, Gerrit	1252
ESTEMAN, Nadab	943
EVERHART, John	2122

EVERIT

Capt. John	449
Lieut. Peter	1381

EVERTS

Oliver	201
Sylvanus	202

EVERY, Joseph	1910
EYERS, Ephraim	2113

FADER (otherwise VEDER)

Lucas	1180
FAIRFIELD, William	1649

FALHAMMER (try 1018)

David	2131

FALKNER

John	1775
Ralph	17,177
William	1607

FARRES, William	908

FARRINGTON (see FERRINGTON)

Robert	1154

FELLERS, George	121

FERGUSON

Alexander	1534
Arra	807
Farrington	806
Israel	803
John	752,2102
Qr. Master John	1665
Peter	1121
Richard	805,1654
Richard Pensioner	204
William	623

FERRIL, Amrist	1694

FERRINGTON (see FARRINGTON)

Stephen	622

FERRIS

John	477
William	1839

FINCLE, George	1648
FINKNER, John	1285
FINNEL, John	1494
FINNEY, Petter	1220

FISHER

Alexander	91
Donald	113
Duncan	93
John	18

FITCHET, Joseph	1500

FITSGERALD/FITZGERALD

John	430
Corpl. John	2017
William	837

FLOCK

Harmanns	100
Harmonus (same?)	1634

FONYA (FONDA?)

Mrs.	520

FORBUSH, Mrs.	624
FOREL, Patrick	463
FORSBURY, John	998
FORSTER, Andrew	466
FORSYTHE, James	172

FOSTER

Adam	1182
David	157
Edward	1177
John	1443

FOX, Fredrick	1321

FRACER (likely FRASER)	
(see FRASER/FRAZER)	
Alexander	380
Daniel	538,1627
Donald	206
James	2182
John	1644
Mrs. John	586
Kenneth/Kennith	778,1774
Thomas	1985
Thomas Junior	1917
Mrs. Thomas	583
William	1645,1984
Mrs. William Snr.	585
Mrs. Capt. William	582
Capt. William	1974
(spelled FRACOR)	
FRALLIN, Michael	1152
FRANCES, Serjt. Jeremiah	2014
FRANKS	
Mrs.	621
William	1549
FRASER (see FRACER/FRAZER)	
Jerimiah	2193
Thomas	1936
Capt. Thomas	2158
William	1930,1938
William	1941,2167
FRATS, Henry	1263
FRAZER, John	1525
FREDRICK	
Brarnd.	1158
Ludwick	1179
FREECE (see FREESE 1436)	
Jacob	1310
FREEL	
Peter	1640
Peter Pensioner	205
FREEMAN	
Peter	1928
Richard	1341
Thomas	1713
FREESE (see FREECE 1310)	
Abraham	1436
FREIDLE, George	407
FRENCH	
Lieut. Gosham	1874
Corpl. Henry	2015
FREOTE (see FRIOT)	
Isac	1658
FRIDAY, Dedrick	106
FRIDRET (FREDRICK?)	
Conrad	2175

FRIOT (see FREOTE)	
Mrs.	539
FROOM, James	769,1760
FROST	
Cloe	178
Edmond	1991
James	848
FRYMIRE	
Nicholas	1465
Philip	1466
FULFORD, Johnathan	824
GALE, Capt. James	491
GALLINGER (see GOLLINGER)	
Hendrick	1415
Michael	1393
GALLOWAY, Benjamin	504
GANTER, Mary	452
GARDNER, John	1512
GARLOCK, Peter	71
GARLOUGH/GARLOW	
John	1736
Jacob	1136
Peter	1210
GARRITT, Robert	89
GATES, Michael	62
GAVIN, James	1777
GAY	
Edward	1146
Rosewell	2096
GERMAN/GERMAIN	
Christopher	698,1999
Jacob	2166
Corpl. John	2029
John Junior	2000
Mrs.	541
GERVEY, John	2092
GIBBINS, Mary	20
GIBSON	
Andrew	208
James	284
John	159,283
Mathew	1480
Thomas	282
GILCHRIST (try 628,2026)	
Peter	2108
GILKER, George	460

GILL, Richard	382	GREEN	
		Benjamin	855
GILLIST, John	1998	Caleb	892
		James	724
GILLOT, Adonigah	1840	John	333
		Rogor	828
GILMAN, Mr. Reverend	1661		
		GREMER, John	1299
GLASFORD			
John	625,1241	GREYHAM, Robert	453
Little	627		
Mrs.	629	GRIFFIN	
		Joseph	753,1682
GLEN, Ensign Jacob	1196	William	836
GOLLINGER (see GALLINGER)		GRIFFS, John	209
Christopher	1426		
George	1173	GRIGGS, Abraham	281
GOLLOWAY, Lt. George	443	GRIMSLEY	
		Charlus	464
GOODMELLY, Joseph	1894	William	465
GOODNIFF/GOODNOFF		GROAT, Henry	1842
John	146		
		GROMMEL, James	692
GOOSBURY, Thomas	1776		
		GRONT, Widow	207
GORDEN			
Robert	381	GROOME	
Serjt. Robert	1520	Elijah	403
		Joseph	406
GORDINER/GORDINIER			
Jacob	1778		
Robert	2106		
		HAASE, George	514
GRAHAM			
Henry	682	HAGERMAN/HEAGERMAN	
John	712	Nicholas	503
Oliver	1016	Tunis	2057
GRAMER, John	1299	HAILS, John	1495
GRANES, Mrs. &		HAIR/HARE	
children (widow)	87	Alexander	714
		Margerit	23
GRANGER, Lachs	901		
		HALL/HALLS	
GRANT (see GRONT)		Archibald	154
Allan	1530	Benyah	388
Angus	1455	James	99
Archibald	334,1119	John	1495
Donald	1213,1528	Richard	397
Duncan	2039		
Finley	1459	HALLENBEEKE/HALLEUBEEKE	
John	400,830,984	Gasbard/Gashard/Gashird	683
Mary	112		
Peter	1212	HALMORE, John	1843
Robert	19		
Widow	207	HAMLIN	
William	868,1514	Mrs.	546
		Silas	1968
GRASS, Capt. Michael	389		
		HAMMER (see 1018)	
GRAY		Col. Conrad	1017
Mrs.	540		
James	2120	HAND, John	1962
John	2019		
Major	1194		
Philip	1516		

HANES			HAWN	
Christian	1445		Harmonus	1369
Joseph & Fambly	84		Hendrick	1410
Michael	1256		John	1368
HANING, Hank	1492		HAYE, William	383
HANLEY/HANLY			HAYOT (try HOYATT/HOYT/HYATT)	
Davis	858		Corpl. Gilbert	2016
Richard	1952			
Rubin	1653		HAYS, Alexander	2047
HARD			HEAGERMAN (see HAGERMAN)	
Eligha	1783		Tunis	2057
Elisha	633			
James	1846		HEART, Bernet	1363
Philo (Philip?)	634			
Phils (Philip?)	1946		HELLIGAR, Serjt. John	1816
Simon	2065			
			HELMER	
HARKIMAN, Danid	1782		Adam	1318
			John	1265,1309
HARLBERT, Moses	909			
			HELTENBRANT/HELDENBRANDT et var	
HARNEY			Jacob	1284
David	2035			
John	707		HENDERSON	
			Archibald	831
HARNS, Josah	976		Caleb	363,1817
			James	850
HARPER, George	410		Peter	285
			William	1123
HARRIS (see HARUS/HERRIUS)				
Gilbert	1006		HENDRICK, Elizabeth	25
Hannah	728			
John	734		HERCHHEIMER/HERKIMAN/HERKIMER	
Jonathan	2001		Mrs.	169
Mrs.	635			
Richard	754,1689		HERMAN, Valentine	1997
HARTEL/HARTLE			HERRIUS (see HARRIS/HARUS)	
Adam	1427		Edward	1296
John	1556			
			HESS, Jacob	1950
HARTMAN, Mrs.	542			
			HEWIT/HEWITT	
HARUS (see HARRIS/HERRIUS)			Henry	1730
Gilbert	973		Barnibus	1731
Johnston	1000			
			HICKEY, John	1138
HARVEY/HARVY (try HARNEY)				
John	707		HICKS (see HIKS/HIX)	
David	364		Lewis	630,1700
			Mrs.	24
HASS, Fredrick	61			
			HIGGINS, Joseph	152
HATCHELLOR, Syx	1913			
			HIGH, William	999
HAULY (see HAWLEY)				
Jadock	2130		HIKS (see HICKS/HIX)	
			Paul	21
HAVENS				
George	214		HILAKER/HILDKER/HILIKER/HILSKER	
John	1929		Jeremiah	545
HAWLEY			HILL, John	897
Abijah	2121			
Isptah	1611		HILLEGAR, Abraham	1784
Jephta	631			
Mrs.	543		HINDMAN, Samuel	215

HINTS, John	865	HOWARD		
		Mathew	1655	
HITTLE, Andrew	697	Mathew Pensioner	374	
HIX (see HICKS/HIKS)		HOYATT (see HAYOT/HOYT/HYATT)		
George	820	Cornelius	2087	
John	822			
Lewis	1700	HOYS, Alexander	2047	

HINTS, John — 865

HITTLE, Andrew — 697

HIX (see HICKS/HIKS)
George — 820
John — 822
Lewis — 1700

HOBSON
Benjamin — 632
Benjimin — 1615

HOFFNOGLE, Mrs. — 549

HOGANS, Edward — 2088

HOGLE
Frances — 22,1616
2100
George — 2022
John — 2021

HOLBERT, Moses — 212

HOLLINBROOKE/HOLUNBROOKE
Samuel — 2089

HOLMES
Elias — 488
John — 401

HOLSTEAD/HOLSTEED
Amos — 1924

HONER, Jaspar — 83

HONSINGER, John — 1288

HOOP, Richard — 1487

HOOPER, John — 210

HOOPLE/HOOPOLE
Hendrick — 1498
John — 1478

HOPPER, Abraham — 1266

HOSIER (try MOSHER/MOSIER)
Joseph — 1943

HOTKINSON, John — 373

HOUGH
Barnabus — 211,1780
Benjamin — 1657
Bruen — 1844
Esia — 1734

HOUGHMAN, Conrad — 929

HOUGHTAIL
Christopher — 2081
Isaac — 2076

HOUSE, Christian — 1268

HOUSINGER, John — 1288

HOWARD
Mathew — 1655
Mathew Pensioner — 374

HOYATT (see HAYOT/HOYT/HYATT)
Cornelius — 2087

HOYS, Alexander — 2047

HOYT (see HOYATT/HAYOT/HYATT)
Abraham — 213

HUBER, Adam — 1340

HUFF
Henry — 1331
Paul — 482

HUFFMAN
David — 1893
Jobest/Johest — 1972
Mrs. — 550
Nicholas — 1963

HUFFNAGLE (see 1821,549)
Jacob — 1779

HUFFNALE (see 549,592,593,1779)
Andrew — 1821

HUFNAIL (try (HOUGHTAIL)
John — 592
Mrs. — 593

HUGDONE, Peter — 1992

HUGGARD, John — 286

HUGUNIER, Daniel — 679

HULIBERT, Philo/Phils — 1620

HUMBERSTONE, Lt. Samuel — 392

HUMPHRY
James — 2168
Mrs. — 589

HUNTER
David — 1981
Moses — 1951

HUNTINGTON, Simon — 544

HUNTLY, John — 1994

HUSTED, Israel — 1171

HUTCHONSON, George — 1919

HUYCH
Lt. John — 677
Togem — 690

HYATT (try HAYOT/HOYATT/HOYT)
Abraham — 1785

INES, Isaac — 911

ITTMAN, Henry	1139
IVES, Isaac	911

JACKSON/JACSON
Henry	756,2101
James	336,2056
John	1819
Thomas	2034

JACOBS, John	1847

JAMES (try JEIMIE)
Darrak	275
Thomas	247

JANNE, Simpson	551
JARSON/JASSON, Henry	756
JEACOCKS, Corpl. David	1386

JEIMIE (try JAMES)
Gilbert	2062

JEROLEMY, James	2141

JESEEP (JESSEEP/JESSUP)
(try JESEPH)
Lt. Col. Ebenezer	1601
Lieut. Edward	1976
Major Edward	1662

JESEPH, Joseph (JESSUP?)	1617

JESSUP (see JESSEP)

JOHNS, Solomon	891

JOHNSON
Charlus	1377
George	1250
Corpl. George	1404
James	636,1934
Corpl. James	1124

JOHNSTON
Hago	176
John	686
William	335

JONAS
Amey	606,1965
Jotmattau	361

JONES
Mrs. Jones's Children	577
Daniel	353
Lieut. David	1663
Ephraim(s)	755,1674
Serjt. James	1471
John	444,729
Capt. John	2023
Capt. Johnathan	1873
Solomon	1667
Thomas	1889,2005
Widow	741
William	726,1971

KANE, Joseph	1737
KELLY, Serjt. Major Martin	1668
KELSEY, James	758,1787
KEMBLE, Barbara	27

KEMP (see KIMP)
James	841
Joseph	847

KENEDY (KENNEDY ?)
Alexander	216
Angus	288
William	26

KENICK, James	287
KERBY, John	289

KETCHEM (see 1440)
Serjt. Ephraim	1726

KIEFF (try OKEEFE/OKIEF)
James	427

KILBURN, Charlus	290
KILMAN, John	1134
KIMP, John	882

KING
Constant	1848
Ebeze	1954
Patrick	1305

KINGSBURY
Joseph	1921
Mrs.	596

KINSHART, Elisha	1735
KINTNER, George	637

KLINE (see CLINE)
Philip	1501

KNANE/KNANES/KNAVE
Adam	1300
John	1302,1849

KNAP
Joseph	757
Serjt. Joseph	2071

KNAPPING, John	910

KNIGHT
James	1258
John	1313
Mealin	153
Rachel	107

KOSINBROOK, Jacob	2097
LAKE, Christopher	1732

LAMPMAN		LOGAN	
Abraham	975,1021	David	338,1890
Abram	2144	James	28
Fredrick	689		
John	1636	LONDON, Assa	217
Peter	685		

LONELESS (see 190)
		Elie	1712
LAMPSON			
John	638,1630	LONG, James	384
Ensign William	2160		

LOSSIE (see 1022)
LANE, John	639,1788	Cornelius	2094

LOSSI (see 2094)
LANGDEN, Richard	1448	Pomps	1022

LASSI (see 2094)
		LOUCKS (otherwise LAUXS et var)	
Pomps	1022	George	1271
		Joseph	1462
LEACH, William	843	Nicholas	2104
		Peter	1433

LEAHY			
John	291	LOUSON, Joseph	1850
William	736,2042		
William Jnr.	352	LOUSSEY, Joshua	2006

LOVELESS (see 1712)
LEAK, Israel	875	Mrs.	190

LEAMAN, John	409	LOW, John	569

LEE, John	393	LUCAS, Daniel	1005

LEEP, John	1955	LYNCH, James	1372,1491

LENNOX, Rowland	2123		

LESTES (see one below)
Thomas	759	MABEES/MABIE	
		(Capt. ?) Abraham	480
LESTOR (see one above)		John	230
Thomas	2082		

		MALLERY	
LEVER, John	218	Elisha	1854
		Enoch	1884
LEWIS, Burrint	725	Jeremiah	1761

LIESON, Daniel	473	MAN/MANN	
		Edward	1508
LIGHT, Benjimin	1964	Isaac	40
		Isaac Junior	1621
LIGHTHART		Isaac Senior	1605
Daniel	553	John	39,1618
John	2084	Ensign Thomas	2011

LINDEY/LINDSEY (see LINSEY)			
James	852,888	MANDAIRD, Richard	1257
John	228,337		
	1690,1740	MANDEVILL, Richard Snr.	1319
LINK			
John	1306	MARKLY (see MERCLE/MERKLEY)	
Mathew	1316	John	1126

LINSEY (see (LINDEY/LINDSEY)			
Darby	227	MARM, Eward	1508
John	1851		

		MARSH	
LIRINS, Tididiah	884	Joseph	898
		William	853,1608
LITTLE, Andrew	376,784	William Pensioner	226
	849		
LIVINGSTON, Serjeant	1202	MARSHELL, John	1337

MARTIN, John   310,1020

MATICE/MATTICE/MATYCE
Henry   1651
Nicholas   1438
Sophy   58

MATTHIAS, John   1295

MAXWELL, William   2196

All the "MAC" Scottish names were
spelled as "M^C" and have been so
transcribed. The spellings vary.

MCACHRON (MCECHREN ?)
Daniel   2040

MCALLUM (MCCALLUM ?)
Peter   360

MCALPIN, Serjt. Duncan   2161

MCARTHUR/MCAURTHER/MCAUTHER
Alexander   854
Charles   840
John   777,839,
                                 1791

MCBAIN/MCBANE
Angus   296
Gillis   1150
Widow   223

MCCALLUM, Peter   360

MCCAN, Alexander   94

MCCARTER,
Donald   1536

MCCARTY
Serjt. Duncan   1522
John   1247

MCCAY (see MCKAY)
Donald   1122
Hugh   1537
James   864

MCCLOUGHERTY, James   1374

MCCONELLY, Hugh   1432

MCCORISTINE, Terence   31

MCCORMACK, William   136

MCCOUNE/MCCOWANE
David   1411

MCCOY, Squire   900

MCCUE
James   1261
William   1287

MCDONALD/MCDONELD
(see MCDONOLD)
Allen   1639
Hugh   562
James   739
John   579,340

MCDONEL
(see MCDONELL/MCDONNEL)
Alexander   1298
Corpl. Alexander   1545
Allan   1529
Angus   29
Corpl. Donald   1523
Donald Senior   1547
Duncan   649
Serjt. Ferquart   1199
Serjt. James   1235
John   643,650
Kenneth   554,1413
Kennith   339
Ketty Junior   36,37
Mrs. (widow)   75
Nelly   38
Serjt. Randel   1402
Renold   79
Reynold   1656
Robert   160
Rodrick   1209

MCDONELL
(see MCDONEL/MCDONNEL)
Alexander   644,1222,
                            1293,1558
Capt. Allen   710
Donald   1559
Donald Junior   1548
Hugh   1552
John   1231,1336,
                            1456,1479
Capt. John   1380
Lieut.   1347
Patrick   1143
Renold   1169

MCDONNEL (see MCDONEL/MCDONELL)
Alexander   1461
Capt. Alexander   1518

MCDONOLD
(see MCDONALD/MCDONELD)
Alexander   2197
Donald   1211
Donold Junior   1214

MCDOUGAL/MCDOUGALL/MCDOUGLE
Alexander   299
Dogal   813
John   1792,1956
Mary   648
Peter   647

MCDOWAL, James   294

MCDUNN, James   470

MCENTIRE
Donald   1137
Duncan   1469
Serjt. John   1198

114

MCENTOSH (see MCINTOSH)		MCKENZIE (continued)	
Alexander	1937	Collin	2018
		Duncan	1324
MCGILLEBRAY, Daniel	1794	Lieut. John	1195
		Lawrence	1010
MCGILLES/MCGILLIS			
Daniel	1435	MCKERNN, William	722
Donald	1535		
Serjeant	1200	MCKIE, Serjt. John	1382
MCGINNIS		MCKIM, James	555
John	716		
Richard	717	MCKINZIE (see MCKENZIE)	
		Collin	220,737
MCGIVIN, (Capt. ?) Daniel	442	John	1120,1908
		Mrs.	594
MCGLAUGHLIN (see 1358)		William	295
William	1407		
		MCKNIGHT, Serjt. Thomas	2028
MCGREGGER (see 783 &			
MCGREGOR/MCGRIGGER)		MCKUNN (MCKEWAN ?)	
Corpl.	1205	William	722
MCGREGOR		MCLARIN (see 651)	
Duncan	125	Mrs.	81
Serjt. Duncan	2163		
Hugh	224	MCLAUGHLEN (see 1407)	
		Alexander	1358
MCGREMER, Mrs.	642		
		MCLEAN	
MCGRIGGER		Danal	1223
(see MCGREGGOR et var)		Mordach	341
Duncan	783	Serjt. Mordoch	1234
MCGRUER, Corpl.	1203	MCLEARDON, Hugh	1543
MCGRUGGER, Peter	1221	MCLEOD, Serjeant	1201
MCHMOYL (?) James	1983	MCLERRAN (see 81)	
		William	651
MCHNOYLE (?) Serjt. Hugh	2013		
		MCMAAUGH, John	2110
MCINLY (MCKINLEY ?)			
Susan	144	MCMARTIN	
		John	358,556
MCINTIRE (see MCENTIRE)		Lieut.	1348
		Malcolm	168
MCINTOSH (see MCENTOSH)			
Donald	33,558	MCMULLEN	
James	221	Daniel	219
John	1003	John	2174
Mary	133	Michael	1333
Mrs.	600		
Mrs. T.	557	MCNAIL, Corpl. Alexander	2030
Peter	292		
		MCNAIRE, Mr.	175
MCKANGHEY/MCKAUGHNEY			
John	1329	MCNAUGHTEN/MCNAUGHTON	
		Donald	1546
MCKAY (see MCCAY)		John	357,1524
Angus	1226		
John	1215	MCNEAL/MCNEIL	
		Archibald	1909
MCKENNY		Mrs.	560
John	1793		
Johns	760	MCNEFF/MCNIFF	
Peter	297	Patrick	711
MCKENZIE (see MCKINZIE)		MCNISH, William	356
Alexander	1790		

MCPHERSON		
Alexander	1527	
John	641,1650,	
	2128	
Keneth	857	
Serjt. Murdock	1521	
Peter	2172	
Widow	561	

MCSHEEHY, Eugene	1852

MCVICAR, Dougal	1251

MCWILLIAMS, Jenny	69

MEAD, James	2077

MEDDOCK, Martin	1398

MELONEY, John	703

MERCLE/MERCLY/MERKLEY	
Fred.	1290
Henry	1272,1286
Jacob	1335
Michael	1275

MERSELIUS, John	1334

MEYERS, Capt. John William	2066

MICHAEL	
David	2147
John	2052

MILHANCH, Peter	139

MILLER	
Adam	785
Andrew	1677
Cornelius	981,1853
Garret	559
Gilbert	298
Jacob	761,913,
	1628
John	838,982
Nicholas	1188
Peter	32
Ralph	222
Thomas	30

MILLIAS, John	1957

MILLS	
Abel	735
Cornelius	1855

MILLUS (MILLS ?)	
John	1957

MINARD, Henry	1789

MITCHELL	
David	2075
George	1307
Winard	1151

MOCK, John	2080

MOFFIT, William	293

MONEY (try below)	
Ambross	416
William	454

MONIER, John	502

MONIES, Captain, Children of	646

MONTROSS, Isaac	123

MORDEN, Lorine	34

MORDICA, Dorn	462

MORDIN	
Daniel	1447
James	1483

MORE	
Frances	914
Hose	2118
Jesper	2063
John	1364
Lieut. Thomas	458
William	499

MOREHOUSE/MORHOUSE	
(see MORKHOUSE)	
John Pensioner	225
William	968

MORKHOUSE, John	810

MORRISON (see 1002)	
Mrs.	645

MOSHER (see MOSIER/HOSIER)	
Benjimin	869
John	395
Lewis	1856

MOSIER (see(HOSIER/MOSHER)	
Christopher	1886
John	1255
Nicholas	2074

MOSS, Serjt. Samuel	1401

MOTT	
Henry	2173
Joseph	1444
Rubin	2203
Mrs. R.	590

MUCHMORE, Mary	179

MULLEN, John	1434

MUNRO	
Daniel	1614
Donald	640
Eliga	912
Elizabeth	131
Hugh	1609
Ensign Hugh	1233
Captain John	1232
Nancy	35
Thomas	128

MURCHSON (see below)
John   1225

MURKESON (see above)
Duncan   1160
John   1277
Mrs.   82

MURPHY, John   1379

MURPORT, Michael   522

MURRISON (see 645)
Johnathan   1002

MURRY
George   1460
Patrick   1166

MUSPORT, Michael   552

MYNARD, Henry   365

NAIL, Fredrick   1172

NAUGHTEN, Andrew Pensioner   229

NEAR, Charlus   1008

NEDO, Lewis   124

NEGROS, Freed (Freed Negros)   523

NELSON
Caleb   342
Calep   2139

NEWTON, John   1246

NICHOLAS, Amey   604

NICHOLASON (see 1949)
Archibald   1697

NICHOL(A)SON (see 1697)
Archibald   1949

NICHOLS
James   1359
John   872,915
Robert   885

NORMAND, Nancy   733

NORTHRIP (see 1942)
Serjt. Elikie   1876

NORTHROP (try 1876,1942)
Mrs.   563

NORTHTRIP (see 1876)
Azur   1942

NORTON
Andrew   1638
Phils (Philip ?)   2151

NOYES, Nathan   925

OAKLY, Benjimin   819

OBLE, Henry   1009

OBREY/OBRYAN/OBRYON (likely
phonetic spellings of O'BRIEN)
John   1390
Mary   300
Timothy   1191

OERA, Philip   862

OGDEN, John   354

OKEEFE/OKIEF (try KIEFF)
Cornelius   1857

OKES, John   1858

O'NEIL, James   762,1619

ONERMOUTH/OVERMOUTH
Lacharah   301

ORR,John   97

ORRA, Philip   862

ORSER, Widow   405

ORSING, John Henry   518

OSBORN/OSBUON/OSBURN
Alexander   104
Israel   103
Nathaniel   2109

OSHOKOKINSEY (an Indian
name ? - or O'SHAUNESSY ?)
Mrs.   652

OSTRANDER
Corpl. Abraham   1980
Everit   2176

OSTWALT, Casper   1007

OUSTERHOUT, Ezekial   519

PADDOCK, John   1450

PALMER
David   812
John   1239
Silas   411

PAPEST (PAPIST ?)
Barnt.   1490

PARK, Cyrenius   966

PARKER, William   41,1859

PARKS
James   896
Nathan   1420
Nathaniel   653,879
Corpl. Robert   1405

PARROTT, Lieut. James	1813
PARRY, William	655
PARTLOW, John	2179
PARTRIGE, Thomas	92
PATERSON/PATTERSON	
Ebenezer	886
George	234,917
Nicholas Junior	428
PEAREAN, Agustine	399
PECK, Calep	1416
PELLS, Henry	918
PENCIL	
John	657
Mrs.	656
PERCY, John	2180
PERRE (PERRY ?)	
John	490
PERRIGO, Serjt. James	1470
PERROT, James	763
PERRY (see 490)	
Robert	654
Corpl. Robert	1758
Samuel	564
William	2129
PERSALS, John	487
PERSON/PERSONS	
Chatwell	2037
Christopher	859
PESCOD, John	1104
PEST, Ensign Harmanus	2068
PETER/PETERS	
Andrew	1795
Lt. Col. John	1752
Ensign John	1754
Samuel	1796
Thomas	771
PETERSON	
Abraham	434
Christopher	433
Serjt. Conrad	1725
Nicholas	431
Paul	432
PITTIT, Dunham	231,1988
PETYEREW (PETTIGREW ?)	
Robert	59
PHELPS, Jonathan	1891

PHILIPS/PHILO/PHILS	
Alinon	834
Elisha	963
John	832
Liba	809
Mary	77
Samuel	916
Sith	818
Thomas	941
PHYLER, Samuel	232
PICKEL/PICKLE	
Christian	827
Jacob	856
John	233,302,826
Peter	787
PICKIN, Mrs.	43
PIERS, William	699
PIKE, Jonathan	935
PITMAN	
Cary	2199
Russel	343,1872
PLACE, Wm. S.	948
PLANT, James	1269
PLASS, Peter	2153
PLATT	
John	1641
Mrs.	80
PLOWTS, John	1297
POOL, George	1902
PORK. John	1898
PORTER/PORTOR	
Benjimin	602
Thimothy	2095
POTHER, William	1419
POWERS, William	385
PRATT, Corpl. John	1475
PRICE	
Barsley	876
Jacob	1304
Thomas	867
PRICHARD/PRICTARD	
A. Junior	953
Agariah	890
PRINGLE	
Doctor	1013
Joel	1019
Joel Senior	1014
Joseph	1015
Timothy	962
William	996

PROCTOR, Ephraim	764,2103	RIENBARRICK, Abram	1679
PROSER, Richard	1360	RILLY (RIELLY ?)	
		David	1278
PRUINER (PRUNER ?)			
Peter	42	RITER, Lieut. John	2067
PURDY		ROACH, John	145
Lt. David	450		
Gilbert	451	ROBERTSON	
		Serjt. Duncan	2012
PURKINS (PERKINS ?)		James	2045
John	863	Joseph	1800
		Thomas	44,1613
PUTMAN/PUTNAM		William	842
Ephraim	1326		
Frances	1391	ROBESON/ROBINSON/ROBISON	
		Daniel	141,658
		James	1243
		Lt. John	459
QUINN		Robert	1417
Christopher	1797	Susana	46
John	1424		
Michael	1423	ROBINS	
		Lieut. James	344,2159
		William	1750
RABBET, Elkanan	1885		
		ROBLEN/ROBLIN	
RADEKER (see 366)		Philip	420
Henry	1860	Owen	425
RANALDS (try REYNOLDS/RYNOLDS)		RODGERS/ROGERS	
Samuel	1506	John	1643
		Major	801
RANE, Joseph	1737	Widow & Mrs.	570
		William	661,1704
RANGIER, William	1187		
		ROKE, John	1798
RAYMOND, Mrs.	660		
		ROSE	
READICK (otherwise REDDICK)		Daniel	1718
George	1267	Mrs. Daniel	568
John	1396	Elizabeth	45
		James	1323
READMAN, Joel	474	Mathew	1799
		Mathias/Matthias	779,1702
REED (see RIED)		Matthias Senior	235
Duncan	90	Samuel	1647
Mrs.	659	Mrs. Samuel	567
		William	1216,1249
REYNOLDS (try RANALDS/RYNOLDS)			
John	861	ROSMAN, Conrad	1881
RICHARDSON		ROSS	
Asa	1659	Drummer Alexander	1387
John	303	Serjt. Charlus	2162
Mrs.	566	Donald	359,1540
Samuel	236,815	Finlay/Finley	130,1412
Thimothy	1739	Jacob	1312
		Linoss	878
RICHMAN, George	2090	Mrs.	588
		Thomas	1230
RICKLEY, Andrew	811		
		ROTHBURN, Josiah	1742
RIDIKER (see 1860)			
Henry	366	ROUGH, James	126
RIED (see REED)		ROUSE, Serjt. George	2070
Cyril	2117		

ROYCE		SCONT (SCOTT ?/SCOUT ?)	
Corpl. Evan	1403	John	1705
Evan	1505		
		SCOTT	
RUDDENBACK, John	2125	Abraham	2170
		Alexander	304
RUE, Fredrick	1376	Daniel	1960
		Mrs. Daniel	572
RUITER		David	1801,1953
Henry	956	Mrs. David	571
John	960	Francis	667
Philip Junior	959	Serjt. Franee	1756
		Neal	1970
RUNNIONS, Henry	1283	Walter	48
RUPORT		SCOUT (SCOTT ?)	
Fredrick	1301	John	345,1705
Peter	1362		1958
		SCUTT (SCOTT ?)	
RUSH, Andrew	825	Alexander	304
RUSSEL/RUSSELL		SEALY, Joseph	239
Elisha	1987		
Stepford	471	SEARON, Christopher	515
William	1105		
		SEE (otherwise CIE et var)	
RUTTIN		David	2200
Captain Peter	418	Harmonus	1716
Lt. William	419	James	664,1698
		John	1687
RYAN, Cornelius	118		
		SEGAR, States	1289
RYKERMAN, John	441		
		SELEE (SEALY ?)	
RYNOLDS (REYNOLDS ?)		Joseph	1805
Jerimiah	949	Justis	1863
		SEMORE/SEMOUR	
		Henry	1517
SALES		Sarah	51
Conrad	102		
Thimothy	1709	SERVICE/SERVOS	
		Christopher/Stophel	1502
SAMPSON			
Aaron	2133	SEYBERT, George	511
Theoph	2134		
		SHADES, Adam	1339
SANDER/SANDERS			
Abraham	2156	SHAFER (see SHAVER)	
Henry Junior	2190	Adam	1108,1174
William	2036,2202	Jacob	394
		John	1165,1270,
SATTERLY, Joseph	1004		1308
		Philip	1111
SAUNDERS			
Mrs.	595	SHARP	
William	2189	Guisbert	1602
		Gusbarts	765
SAVER, John	1181	John	1745,1923
		Corpl. Philip	2164
SAWYER, John	1513		
		SHAVER	
SCHAMORHORN/SCHAMSHORN		George	1178
William	1633	Jacob	1184
		Marchus	1457
SCHERP, John	680		
		SHAW	
SCHILLING, John	49	Mr.	517
		Robert	472

SHEETS (otherwise SCHEETS/
SCHEIKS)
George   1129
Jacob   1206,1446
William   1355
(Where is CHRISTIAN SHEETS who was
allotted land in Second - Cornwall
- Township, V/w25, on McNiff's
1786 map.)

SHELL, John   1320

SHERER (see 665)
Thomas   2194

SHERMAN/SHERMON (same person
- one family ?)
Simeon   662
Simon   1803

SHEROR (see 2194)
Thomas   665

SHERWOOD
Capt. Justus   1812
Moses   115
Rubin   2157
Samuel   367,1862
Thomas   266
Ensign Thomas   1875

SHIBLEY, Corpl. John   2031

SHOOLS, John   1170

SHOREY, Mrs.   668

SHORT, Rosana   101

SHORTY, John   1959

SHOUGHNESSEY, William Henry   2152

SHRADER, Magunws   1722

SHUFFET, Henry   2148

SHURR, Peter   2192

SILLICK, Darby   1915

SIMONS/SIMMONS
Baltis   1710
Daniel   1947
Lieut. Henry   1753
John   1707
Serjt. John   1670
Moses   1747
Mr.   174
Nicholas   78
Titus   766,1622

SIMPSON
Janne   551
Robert   241
Serjt. Robert   2069

SINGER, John   50

SINITGAR (SNITTSINGER ?)
Philip   1820

SKIMMING, Mary   47

SKINKLE, Henry   1691

SLETER (SLATER ?)
William   1861

SMITH (see SMYTH)
Alexander   455
Comfort   243,877
Daniel   479,816
Elias   114
Eliphet   347
Elipholet   873
Ensign   1102
George   704,1510,
                                1666
Henry   817
John   240,2111
Serjt.   John   1400
Joseph   309
Patrick Esquire   188
Philip   2098
Richard   421,1259
Robert   375,1804
Samuel   242
Stephen   386
William   127,2020

SMYTH (see SMITH)
Benonea   238
Dinnis (Dennis ?)   1706
Serjt. John   1978
John Tory   237

SNETTSINGER/SNITTSINGER
(try 1820)
Mathias   1291

SNIDER (see SNYDER)
Adam   1130
Zachary   1686

SNYDER (see SNIDER)
Abraham   2033
Christian   995
Conrad   1117
Isaac   1721
Jacob   671
Jeremiah   1452
John   1993
Marks   1711
Mrs.   591
Peter   2041
Simon   669,1888
William(s)   767,1624,
                                1675

SOLES, William   1802

SOLOMON, Jeremiah   1292

SOMERS (see SUMMERS)
Andrew   1218

SPEED, George   919

SPENCER		STONE	
Benjimin	950	James	1806
Edward	871	Simon	2044
Jeremiah	952		
Peleek	955	STONEBURNER (see STEINBURNER)	
Serjeant	1348	Jacob	1294
Thomas	951	John	1477
		Corpl. Jos.	1544
SPICER		Drummer Leanerd	1388
Daniel	2048		
Ezekial, Jnr. & Snr.	346,2003, 2049	STONEMAN, Nicholas	135
		STONER, Martin	663
SPOONER, Ralph	244		
		STORM/STORMS	
SPRINGFIELD, Michael	417	Gilbert	666,1990
SPRUNG, Volkert	691	STORRING (STARRING ?)	
		John	1399
SRIVER, George	1175		
		STOVER, Martin	1899
STAAT (otherwise STATA/STATE)			
Robert	308	STRADER	
		Henry	1156
STAFFORD, Joseph	1733	John	1157
STANLY, Matty	64	STREET, Samuel	1489
STARNS (try 870)		STREIGHT	
Nathaniel	96	Ludwick Junior	719
		Ludwick Senior	718
STARS, George	2171		
		STUARD (see STEWARD)	
STATA/STATE (see STAAT)		John	149
Henry	1327	William	140,306
Philip	1394		
		STULL, Andress	581
STAUTS, Corpl.	1361		
		STURNS (STERNS ?; try 96)	
STAYGE, William	424	Simier	870
STEEL, Mathew	422	SULFRAGE, John	2146
STEINBURNER (see STONEBURNER)		SULLIVAN	
John	1477	Cornelius	1357
		Dennis	1338
STENBERGER, Jacob	732		
		SUMMERS (see SOMERS)	
STENBERGH, Stephen	1253	Corpl. Jacob	1352
STENEBRANDER, John	1477	SUTHERLAND	
		James	307
STEPFORD, Russel	471	Mrs.	63
STEVENS, Roger	1652	SUTTON, Samuel	1373
STEVENSON, John	1604	SUURR, Peter	2192
		(The name SURR/SORRE is to be found	
STEWARD (try STUARD)		in Yorkshire, England around	
David	670	Pocklington; Parish of Hayton and	
Solomon	829	village of Bielby in 1760s.)	
STILL, John	776,1701	SWARTS, Simon	1141
STILLWILL, Obediah	445	SWATT, Simon	413
STOCKS, Adam	119	SWEET	
		Nicholas	954
STOGLELON/STOGHELON		Oliver	305,1818
Henry	1781		

TAISON, Jaimes	1786		TUTTLE (continued)	
			William	1714
TAYLOR				
Alexander	311		TYLER/TYLOR	
Michael	414		Jerid	1887
Peter	893		Mrs.	573
			William	957
TEEPLE, John	1103			
TELLEBOCK				
Bellshazzer/Bellshazger	1451		ULMAN, Frances	1328
TERRY, Amy	85		UPTON, William	1011
TEWHEY, John	1153		URQUART, William	1464
THITTLE, Andrew	697			
THOMAS				
Corpl. Jacob	2073		VALENTINE	
James	247		Benjamin	495
Peter	2058		Gabriel	2132
			Herman	1997
THOMPKINS, Israel	1695		Isac	2093
			John	2150
THOMPSON			Ensign John	1519
Corporal	1237			
Jacob	248,1883		VALDE, Lt. Peter	481
John	881,1148			
Mathew/Mathews	768,1681		VAN ALLEN	
William	860		Corporal	1238
			John	1606
THORNE, John	507			
			VAN CAMP	
TIBERE, Joseph	52		Jacob	2050
			James	1109
TICHONT, William	246		Jamis (JAMUS ?)	2051
			John	1996
TILLINBACK, Henry	521		Peter	68
			Simon (see 2043)	70,348
TIMMER, William	110			
			VAN DE BOGART, Frances	887
TINKEL, Corpl. Henry	1879			
			VAN KOUGHNET/COUGHNET	
TINKEY, Abraham	2053		John	111
TOBARGE, John	987		VAN VORST	
			John	54
TOEHOUT, William	2184		Yellis	821
TOWNBULL, Andrew	730			
			VANALSTINE (see ESELTINE)	
TOWNER, Athill	312		Isac	1224
			Lanl.	1144
TRIP, Robert	770,2140		Marg.	164
			Mrs.	72
TRUMBLE, Asahell	1864		Captain Peter	676
TUNGATE, Robert	713		VANDEKER, Rudoff	55
TURNER, Richard	1939		VANDERHIDER, Adam	2187
TUTTLE			VANDERLAP/VANDERLEP/VANDERLIP	
John	1688		Fredrick	675
Joseph	1916			
Nathaniel	1926		VANDUSON	
Solomon	1454		Gaspard	727
Stephen	672,1632,		Conrad	723
	1715			
Widow	245		VANGANT, John	969

VANHORN	
Cornelius	696
Richard	693
VANSKREVER, Peter	695
VANZANT, John	969
VELEI, Andrew G.	1845
VELES Philip G.	1841
(above two the same?)	
VENNOR, Michael	1370
VENT/VINT, Adam	772,1807
VON STEINBERG, Stephen	1253
WAGER, Everhart	2083
WAGGONER	
Frances	163
Jacob	1409
WAIDE, Corpl.	1236
WAIDRAD, Jacob	1869
WAINSWRIGHT, John	1808
WAIT	
George	142
James	387
John	57
WAITER, Philip	1342
WAKLEY, Stephen	921
WALDENBROCK, John	492
WALDRAD, Jacob	1869
WALDROFF, Marg.	56
WALKER, Daniel	774,1810
WALL, Daniel	1748
WALLICE/WALLIS	
James	1449
Serjeant	1349
WALLISCER	
Anthony	1183
Martin	1161
WALTER, Martin	1159
WARD	
Able	1746
Serjt. John	1815
WARDNER, Thomas	930

WARNER	
John	970
Levi	936,983
WARRING, Fredrick	1811
WARTMAN, Mrs.	587
WASBURN/WASHBURN	
Serjt. Ebenzer	1977
Mrs.	587
WATSON	
Aron	2046
Major	143
Mathew	997
Ralph	250
WAYWOOD, Thomas	255
WEARTHEAD, Samuel	2105
WEAVER	
Fredrick	1131
John	1142
WEBSTER, Milo	2007
WEED, Corpl. Obijah	1125
WEHN/WEHR, Lt. Christian	257
WEIST, John	773
WELSH	
Samuel	256
Thomas	1866
WERT	
Andrew	1482
Conrad	1481
John	1132
WEYMIRE, George	2135
WHALING, Michael	1497
WHALLEN, Michael	1870
WHETMAN (see 349)	
Robert	1961
WHITE	
Captain Alexander	500
Joseph	1867
Joseph Junior	1871
Samuel	2064
William	1912
WHITLEY, John	1920
WHITMAN (see 1961)	
Robert	349
WHORRING, Dennis	478
WICKWIRE	
Jonathan	1868
Libious/Livious	814

WIES, David	109	WITMAN (try WHITMAN)		
		George	978	
WIEST, John	2183			
		WOGHUFF, John	2191	
WILKINSON/WILKISON				
(see WILLISTON)		WOLENT, Mrs.	65	
Donald	165			
		WOOD		
WILLIAMS		John	76,313	
Armstrong	2169		1560	
Serjt. David	1878	Jones	1375	
Fredrick	508	Thomas	1865	
John	674,1809	Widow	253	
Corpl. John	1671			
Mosses	967	WOODBURN, John	1940	
Mrs.	673			
		WORMWOOD, William	1425	
WILLISTON, William	1918,1935			
		WORRICK, James	2149	
WILLS, William	476			
		WORT, George	1551	
WILMOTT, Antony	505			
		WRAFF, Richard	249	
WILSON				
Edward	429	WRIGHT		
John	1629	Ebenezer	252	
Mrs.	574	Samuel	251	
		Widow	412	
WILTSE/WILTSIE		William	1751	
Benonie	1749			
Benoni	254			
Serjt. Benonee	1669	YORK/YORKS		
James	1880	Daniel	2137	
		Isac	440	
WIMP, Arom	868			
		YOUNG		
WINTER		Alexander	258	
Elizabeth	161	Henry	575	
George	1228	James	132	
Henry	86	John	985	
WITHERWAX, William	2099